ISLAND
ENCOUNTERS
TIMOR-LESTE FROM THE OUTSIDE IN

ISLAND ENCOUNTERS

TIMOR-LESTE FROM THE OUTSIDE IN

LISA PALMER

MONOGRAPHS IN
ANTHROPOLOGY SERIES

Australian
National
University

PRESS

For my mother and for Quin

ANU PRESS

Published by ANU Press
The Australian National University
Acton ACT 2601, Australia
Email: anupress@anu.edu.au

Available to download for free at press.anu.edu.au

ISBN (print): 9781760464509
ISBN (online): 9781760464516

WorldCat (print): 1257518587
WorldCat (online): 1257503196

DOI: 10.22459/IE.2021

Cover design and layout by ANU Press. Cover image: 'Wai Lia', Lino Print by Celia Mira, Afalyca Art Centre, Baucau.

Contents

List of Maps   ix

List of Photographs   xi

Acknowledgements   xv

Prologue   xvii

Introduction   1

1.   The Not-So-Wild West   17

2.   Enclave Society   29

3.   Back Across the Border   45

4.   Courting Bees in a Divided Land   55

5.   The Politics of *Lulik*   71

6.   Small Island Sojourns   83

7.   Underground Flows   95

8.   Ritual and Recovery   111

9.   Life in the Rice Fields   125

10. 'The Geographical Tour'   143

11. Carrying the Name Forward   157

12. Opening the Paths to Healing   169

13. New Beginnings   183

Epilogue   193

Glossary of Language and Terms   201

Audiovisual Resources   205

Further Reading   207

List of Maps

Map 1: Map of island Timor and journey from west to east.   xx

Map 2: Location of Lookeu, one of the five kingdoms
       of Koba Lima.   57

Map 3: Wai Lia Bere's asserted underground flows and spring
       connections.   97

List of Photographs

Photo 1: *Tais* purchased in Dili, 1997.   xviii

Photo 2: Sunrise at Jaco.   4

Photo 3: Rice fields and mountains in the kingdom of Lookeu.   18

Photo 4: View from Biboki highlands towards Oecusse.   24

Photo 5: The main palace at Tam Kesi.   26

Photo 6: Honeycomb in the megaliths of Tam Kesi.   26

Photo 7: Zeca and puppy with friends in the rice fields.   35

Photo 8: Noefefan Bridge, Oecusse.   37

Photo 9: Monument to the Portuguese arrival, Lifau.   38

Photo 10: *Liurai* Antonio da Costa outside his Pante Makasar house (with author).   40

Photo 11: Rosa making earthenware pots.   42

Photo 12: Oecusse's main international border.   46

Photo 13: Graves of the former king of Ambeno, Joao da Cruz, and his wife, Maria da Cruz.   47

Photo 14: East Timorese 'garden house' in Atambua village.   53

Photo 15: The palace of Uma Metan Lookeu.   61

Photo 16: Ritual inside Uma Metan Lookeu.   62

Photo 17: A *laku* begins his climb.   64

Photo 18: The black stone basket offering.   65

Photo 19: Honey harvest fire blooms.   67

Photo 20: Straining the honey.   68

Photo 21: Flag house with painted Australian flag in Balibo.   72

Photo 22: View from Balibo Fort.   73

Photo 23: The channel between Jaco (Tortina) and mainland Timor-Leste.   80

Photo 24: Women sewing inside Boneca de Atauro.   84

Photo 25: Quin and Jose.   87

Photo 26: Atauro coastline.   89

Photo 27: Cape Bondura coastline, Baucau.   90

Photo 28: Maria and her medicine cabinet.   92

Photo 29: Buffalo and herder on the Baucau plateau.   98

Photo 30: *Kabu bee* and rice farmers maintaining the irrigated water channels.   101

Photo 31: Wai Lia spring pool and government pump station.   103

Photo 32: Main road, Darasula.   114

Photo 33: Simiao and final water blessing.   118

Photo 34: Offering inside Wai Lia Bere cave.   118

Photo 35: Simiao's father at medicinal tree.   122

Photo 36: Rice harvest ritual offering.   126

Photo 37: Wai Daba rice fields with Mt Ariana in background (Old Man at right).   128

Photo 38: Tia Martina carries out her part of the rice harvest offering.   133

Photo 39: Lunch in Noyti's rice fields.   135

Photo 40: Madalena and Golden.   138

Photo 41: The purchased pig.   140

Photo 42: The 50-cent swing beach.   148

Photo 43: Students at Iralalaru and the Irasiqiru river (Demetrio speaking with Senhor Hermingildo standing at rear).   151

Photo 44: The Old Lady in her rice fields.   163

Photo 45: Januario's clinic with Salvador and his father.   171

Photo 46: Palmira pounding forest medicine. 173

Photo 47: Collected bones and soil in their sarongs. 175

Photo 48: Making the burial coffins. 176

Photo 49: The 23 grave compartments. 179

Photo 50: Carrying the grasses into the house reconstruction site. 184

Photo 51: The parent house reconstruction site with Matebian
mountains in the background. 185

Photo 52: Offerings to the sacra. 187

Photo 53: The Old Man walking through rice fields. 190

Photo 54: View from our house. 194

Photo 55: Cooking *katupa* by the kitchen. 195

Photo 56: The Old Man carrying out a ritual at the Ocabai
spring source. 196

Acknowledgements

Island Encounters has had a long gestation and there are a great many people to thank and acknowledge. My deepest thanks go to my extended family from across the island of Timor and my own family here in Australia. I have been privileged to be welcomed into their lives and to learn and benefit from the qualities they have shared: inclusivity, warmth, joy in the company of others, and an enthusiasm for extending out a seemingly endless network of family, friendships and stories.

For their love and companionship, I thank my husband Quintiliano Mok and our children Madalena and Zeca. A huge debt of gratitude to all our family in Baucau and Bercoli and to Balthasar Kehi and his family from the dispersed kingdom of Lookeu. I thank all those Timorese we encountered on this journey and who shared with us so generously their hospitality and insights. In particular, I acknowledge the unwavering support and encouragement of Celastinu Freitas and Fransisco Almeida, my long-term research collaborators in Baucau. I thank too the various individuals, communities and community organisations who have hosted me over the years across the Baucau and Viqueque municipalities and in Tutuala, Maubisi, Fatumean and Dili.

I acknowledge and thank an inspirational network of colleagues from Timorese civil society organisations and from universities in Timor-Leste, Australia and across the world. This book would not have been possible without my engagement over two decades with these people. In particular, I thank Demetrio do Amaral de Carvalho, Pedro Viera and Joanna Soares from the Haburas Foundation and those academics with whom I have spent varied amounts of 'field' time together inside Timor-Leste: Balthasar Kehi, Susanna Barnes, Andrew McWilliam, Josh Trindade, Sara Niner, Ritsuko Kakuma, Teresa Hall, Marcia Langton, Alex Cullen, Antonio Vicente Marques Soares, Simon Batterbury, Thomas Reuter, Lucas da

Costa, Russell Drysdale and Sue Jackson. For their wise counsel and support at various times, I thank Marcia Langton, Abel Guterres, David and Maxine Hicks, and James Fox.

For their close and considered reading of initial drafts or extracts of this manuscript, I thank my mother Jenni Wells, my stepfather Graeme Wells, Susanna Barnes, Balthasar Kehi, Sara Niner, Kirsty Sword Gusmao, Andrew McWilliam, Bu Wilson and Gordon Peake.

For his enthusiasm and support I thank Matt Tomlinson, managing editor of the anthropology series at ANU Press. I also thank ANU Press's deputy manager Emily Tinker, and Rani Kerin for her copyediting. For her kindness and map work over many years, I thank Chandra Jayasuriya. For permission to reproduce the cover image, I acknowledge and thank the artist Celia Mira and the assistance of the Afalyca Art Centre in Baucau and the Box Hill Community Arts Centre in Melbourne. Thank you to Seth Keen for design advice.

For funding support, I acknowledge two Australian Research Council Discovery Grants (DP1095131 and DP160104519) and the support of a fellowship from the Firebird Foundation for Anthropological Research. The School of Geography at the University of Melbourne supported my sabbatical in 2018 and I acknowledge the collegiality of the school and the leadership of Lesley Head who is always encouraging us to reach wider audiences.

My final thank you is to Tamsin Wagner, whose expertise and editorial guidance from the outset until the very end of this writing process has been essential to the life of *Island Encounters*. Without our many and varied conversations, her enthusiasm, ever patient and considered prompts, editing, advice and encouragement, this book would not have come to fruition.

A version of Chapter 4 was previously published in the 2019 summer edition of the *Meanjin Quarterly*. Short extracts from Chapters 7, 8 and 12 have been published in articles in *Asia Pacific Viewpoint* and *The Australian Journal of Anthropology* (details in Further Reading).

Lisa Palmer
Melbourne
June 2021

Prologue

The first time I visited (East) Timor, I was there for an hour. The passenger ferry I was travelling on through the eastern Indonesian archipelago had docked just long enough for me to jump in a waiting taxi and do some shopping. I wanted to buy *tais*—the famous Timorese woven cloth. Yet, as we drove to the local handicrafts shop, I felt a little unnerved. The streets were near deserted, eerily so. There was not a tourist in sight, and the local people stared at me blankly. Still, the owner of the handicrafts shop greeted me enthusiastically. I looked through the piles of cloth he had on display and chose a boldly coloured one with Portuguese-inspired patterning, a design that marked it out from all the Indonesian *ikat* cloth I had seen elsewhere.

Engrossed in my choice of cloth, I didn't notice that the taxi driver was hovering around me nervously. He was anxious to get going. When we arrived back to the docks, I found out why! The ferry was pulling off its mooring and the gangplank was already raised. Yet the sight of a 20-something white girl stranded alone by a taxi on the docks was enough to bring the captain round. He returned the ship back to its mooring and the gangplank was lowered. As I boarded, a battalion of on-rotation Indonesian troops cheered me on wildly. I was horrified at having created a spectacle. The ship set sail and I found a place to hide on the upper deck.

It was from there in 1997 that I first studied island Timor. From my vantage point, I stared earnestly out across the water at the windy narrow coastal roads and stony dry river mouths that dotted the coastline. This land was full of its own horror, I knew. But from this distance it gave little away.

More than 20 years on, I can read the twists and turns on those narrow coastal roads and I am familiar with the names and origins of those many stony coastal rivers. I have heard many of the stories that follow the turns on these roads and that accompany the intermittent flows of the rivers. I have also come to know much more about the pain and the joy that infuses the cultural depths of the entire Timorese landscape.

Photo 1: *Tais* **purchased in Dili, 1997.**

Map 1: Map of island Timor and journey from west to east.

Source: Chandra Jayasuriya.

Introduction

This book tells a story of how I have come to know island Timor and, ultimately, why I think these understandings matter. It's a story I tell in snapshots from a six-month journey in 2018 with my family as we travelled from one end of the island to the other (see Map 1). It is a story of personal encounters with people who call Timor their home and of encounters with the landscape itself. And, given that this is an island divided, that story of division is one I must also tell.

Like the cloth or *tais* I bought on my first visit to the country, this is a story told by the threading together of the warp and weft. The lengthwise 'warp' dwells in the experiences of the two decades of my involvement with Timor-Leste and, more particularly, the months I spent travelling with my family from west to east across the island. The crosswise 'weft' is made up of the stories and ideas that shuttle back and forth across the island to create the shared fabric of Timorese people's lives. These often deeply cultural stories and ideas weave and continually reweave together the past, present and future. They connect not only the people but also the languages, lands, waters, animals and plants that comprise this rich and varied landscape. These are reoccurring stories across time and space that are suffused with ideas about the profound life-organising significance of insiders and outsiders, the mountains and the sea, the trunks and the tips, the darkness and the light, family and marriages, traditions and modernity. The threads of these diverse preoccupations cultivate and nurture relationships, revealing layered interconnections between people and the land and an astonishing depth of historical attentiveness. While these stories and their spread across the island are the core concerns of the book, in this introduction I first sketch some of the history of my involvement with Timor-Leste. I then address a topic that so often encases, masks, foils or even brings these deeper cultural stories to the fore: the paradoxes of development.

***

After my first fateful visit to Timor in 1997, I returned to Australia to complete my postgraduate studies on Indigenous ownership of Kakadu National Park. Then, in 1999, when I was still a student in Darwin, the East Timorese gained the miraculous right to vote in a referendum—to choose whether they wanted to stay with Indonesia or cut their ties and become an independent nation-state. They chose the latter option, and resoundingly so. When the Indonesian state followed suit and withdrew from the territory, its military and their civilian militia burnt most of the tiny half island to the ground. Those Timorese that could, fled in horror.

Some of them came to Darwin. My doctoral supervisor, Marcia Langton, rallied her networks including the then head of the Northern Territory's Aboriginal Medical Service, Pat Anderson. Together our group set up a makeshift refugee emergency centre. In the centre, those arriving from East Timor found camaraderie and access to the services they needed. The refugee families were deeply traumatised and in desperate need of reprieve. When Marcia and I went to fetch them from the motel where the refugees were being housed by the government, we found it was being decked out in red and white streamers. Red and white are the colours of the St George Rugby Club, a team who had made it to that weekend's grand final in Sydney. The motel owners bragged that they had now converted the Timorese refugees into St George supporters. Yet these colours were also the colours of the Indonesian flag—*merah putih* 'the red and the white'—a political symbol that the murderous Indonesian military had literally forced the Timorese to swear allegiance to over 24 brutal years. Marcia, an Indigenous Australian who knows well the everyday effects of lingering colonialisms and insensitivities, was incensed and pointed out the unfortunate coincidence to the motel owners. They couldn't see the problem. Marcia recalls the Timorese simply shrugged at her with resignation. What could they do?

Marcia had been to Timor before. In 1991, when the occupied territory had first started to open up to the outside world, she had travelled there with a nun on a humanitarian mission. In her 2001 Overland Lecture 'Senses of Place', delivered at the Trades Hall in Melbourne, she had reflected on her experiences in East Timor and on the similarities and differences between the Indigenous Australian and Timorese fight against colonialism and for self-determination. She recalled how, in this first visit to East Timor, people spoke with her very little; they were too scared.

Yet she saw in their eyes the all too familiar gaze of a people subjected to colonialism and almost unspeakable shame and horror. She also recognised their determination to continue to fight, and the depth of faith they had in themselves and their traditions. Participating one Sunday in a Catholic mass delivered by the Nobel Peace Prize–winning Timorese Bishop Dom Carlos Belo, she and the other attendees steeled themselves against the whirr of two Indonesian military helicopters that were intent on intimidating the parishioners from above. As Marcia explained:

> We wondered, as I am sure the parishioners did, if the Indonesian military would burst out of their spiteful airborne strategy and start shooting. And it was then that I understood that if they did, it would not matter. And this was the point of spirituality and culture: the protection these provide is simply a knowledge that self-respect is as important as all other virtues.

Marcia visited the territory for a second time in the immediate wake of the 1999 referendum. She was there for a language conference and the leaders of the freed territory were trying to agree on a workable language policy for the new nation. While the political elite had been educated in Portuguese, a newer generation of budding politicians and academics were educated in Indonesian. Both languages were vying for political ascendancy. Alongside the lingua franca, Tetum, most people additionally spoke one or more of Timor's more than 30 indigenous languages.

Language policy was and remains a flashpoint issue in the tiny nation. Used often as a tool to wield power and status, divergent views can trigger deep recriminations and anger on all sides. While Portuguese and Tetum eventually became the new country's designated official languages, with Indonesian and English as working languages, the status and recognition of indigenous languages has been more opaque. Amid at times controversial public debates, some Timorese have forcefully continued to assert colonial ideas that consider indigenous languages to be backward or unsuited for the modern world. Some raise concerns about the potential for the official indigenous language policies to divide rather than unite the country. Others have more mundane concerns, and some parents who are fluent in indigenous languages—but who worry about their children's educational future—ban indigenous languages from being spoken at home. A minority of public advocates are more supportive: they recognise that the majority of rural Timorese primarily speak one or more of these indigenous languages at home and they have advocated for these languages to be recognised in the national curriculum.

Language is, of course, not the only controversial post-independence issue. So, too, in the early years was the status and role of diaspora Timorese, many of whom were returning to help rebuild their country after spending a large part of the occupation overseas. In late 2000, Marcia and I were invited to visit Timor-Leste by Hilario Goncalves, our friend and karate teacher in Darwin. Hilario—or Sensei, as we called him—was a compassionate and highly skilled diaspora Timorese who had long lived in Darwin where he worked as a draftsman on remote Aboriginal community housing. In late 1999, after the United Nations had taken control of the still smouldering territory, Hilario had seized the chance to return to his homeland. There he worked as a United Nations (UN) volunteer in the Land and Property Unit, helping them for more than a year as they tried to piece his country back together. He was also slowly piecing his own family and his place in it back together. When Marcia and I visited, Hilario hired a car and drove us eight hours to visit some of his family in Fuiloro in the far east of the island. When we descended from there to the coast on the eastern tip, I thought we might have entered paradise. We found ourselves in a tiny fisher's camp replete with pandanus-fringed squeaky white sands and crystal-clear waters. Tropical forest ran from the mountains to the sea. A little island called Jaco beckoned from across the strait.

Photo 2: Sunrise at Jaco.

When he had arrived back in Timor after the referendum, Hilario had mostly lived and worked in Dili. By the time we visited him there in late 2000, he was deeply disillusioned. His homecoming had been sweet, but a bitterness was creeping in. He had seen the UN at its best and at its worst, only the sting of the latter was now prevailing. The waste, the opportunism, the cultural blindness, the exclusions faced by Timorese people and, above all, the sheer madness of the bureaucracy were breaking him. The UN, he said, treated his country like it had no leaders, rules or laws of its own. For them, he implied, Dili (where most UN personnel were headquartered and rarely left) was like the lawless Wild West. He had decided to leave. 'I'll come back once they are gone,' he said.

So, Hilario returned to Darwin. The UN mission stayed in Dili, 'managing' the country on and off until 2012. When they finally left, it was not without a legacy. While other diaspora Timorese stayed on, later filling important positions in the new government and bureaucracy, their re-entry into the country at the time of a bloated UN and aid economy saw many of them tarnished by their fellow countrymen and women as opportunists. Even the fiercest supporters of independence were at times lumped in with those who had vocally supported Indonesian rule and who, much to the chagrin of those who stayed, had now returned to enjoy the benefits of independence. In many cases, which 'side' people took through a long and tortuous occupation was neither clear cut nor fully knowable. All these issues continue to simmer in the background of Timorese politics and everyday life.

***

Following my first visit to an independent Timor-Leste in the year 2000, I began to visit the country regularly from 2004. In the intervening period I had moved to work at the University of Melbourne and married a man I had met in the Melbourne suburbs—a Timorese man called Quintiliano Mok. While I have since carried out long-term academic research in the country, it is the experiences of travelling to Timor-Leste with Quin and spending longer periods of time with his extended family in the eastern region of the country that has most profoundly shaped my sense of Timor-Leste.

Much of this time has been spent in the country's second city of Baucau in a home shared by Quin's father, many of his children and grandchildren. In these experiences, the figure of my father-in-law, now deceased, looms large. My father-in-law, Jose Maria Mok Kingsang, was of Timorese-Chinese descent; his own father had arrived in Baucau from China and married a local woman from the Baucau hinterland sometime around the turn of the twentieth century. In 1974, soon after the Indonesians first invaded, Jose fled to the mountains to become a guerrilla in FALINTIL, the East Timorese resistance force. In the late 1970s, when the East Timorese resistance leaders decided that they had no choice but to encourage a mass civilian surrender, it was Jose who bravely led down countless starving families from their mountain hideouts to the town of Baucau. He was then jailed and tortured for many months, subjected to the same treatment that had earlier been inflicted on his eldest son Domingos in retribution for his father's resistance activities in the jungle. During that period, the twelve-year-old Quin took on the role of delivering food daily to his father in prison and was forced to witness despicable acts of torture.

Later in the Indonesian era, my father-in-law opened a restaurant on the family's sprawling property in a central part of Baucau. At considerable personal risk, he lived a double life, hosting Indonesian military commanders in the restaurant while securing an urban hideout and meeting place for FALINTIL resistance guerrillas out the back. It was there in 1991 that Marcia first met my future father-in-law.

***

Two years after Quin and I were married in a small gathering in my mother's garden in Tasmania, we held a much larger wedding at Jose's home in Baucau. Quin was made an Australian citizen and we began travelling to Timor-Leste frequently. We eventually had children and, together with Quin, I began carrying out research across the Baucau region. During this time, I slowly began to notice a pattern in the way people would treat me. While we never foregrounded our family ties, the people we met were always very keen to establish who we 'really' were. Once people had found out who Quin's father was, they would suddenly open up. Most often they would find some kind of extended family connection between us. Sometimes it would turn out that they, or one of their family members, had actually attended our wedding. In turn, their worlds opened up to me.

The encounters and experiences I have had as a result of these family connections, this journey from the outside in, are not stories I find in other accounts of Timor-Leste. Neither are they things I have previously written or spoken about much myself. The encounters enabled through this kind of hyper-networked social world are not easily translated to my everyday experiences of life in urban Australia.

Family life in Timor-Leste is busy; there are always a myriad of extended family rituals and other gatherings to plan for or to attend, and some kind of intra-family crisis is never far away. People across large networks gather frequently to get married, commiserate, argue, fight, mourn, negotiate and celebrate. Ancestral communication and rituals need to be continually attended to, patronage networks must be cultivated, crops need to be sown and harvested, and resources, including property rights, must be carefully monitored and manoeuvred for. Within an extended household, there is very often tension, especially between siblings and their families, and sometimes the potential for violence. Frequently in such large family groupings unexpected pregnancies occur, adding both joy and burden to the lives of those caring for the large numbers of children already present in the household. All of these events are larger than the individuals concerned, drawing in transgenerational groupings that span extended families spread out across the country, the entire island, other countries and even continents. Given all this, I have never felt the need to leave Jose's family property in Baucau to feel a deep and immediate connection with the wider world.

This is not an optional social world nor is it always satisfactory, but neither is it, for me, too onerous or forced—it simply spirals and unfolds. When things go wrong, whether it be a death or a car breakdown on remote roads, these family networks swing seamlessly into action. There are always multiple people on hand to call for assistance or support and somehow it always seems possible to mobilise quickly the necessary skills to resolve an urgent circumstance. Even, or especially, in more dire situations, it is this familial and collective capacity to pull together and mobilise that continually surprises me.

Immediately upon arriving in Timor-Leste, I feel arising in me a slower sense of being. Before long, this slowness will merge with a liveliness as I am once again engrossed in activities of Timorese life: traversing its diverse landscapes, moving with the threads and knots of tightly packed kin relations and negotiating pathways through the subtly interwoven worlds of deep custom and modern aspiration. The richly networked cares and concerns of Timorese life will once again intervene and take over my everyday world.

These familial experiences are, in many ways, both central to and a world away from the capital Dili and its preoccupations with development politics, nation and capacity building. After freeing itself materially from the shackles of the Indonesian occupations and a much longer history of Portuguese colonialism, Timor-Leste became emblematic as the world's newest nation-state and associated nation-building processes. Yet, in the minds of many, these histories linger only too deeply. When the UN took control from 1999–2002, plans were hatched immediately to usher in a new democracy through free and fair party political elections and to put in place new techno-bureaucratic systems. By the time the Timorese were able to assert effective control over their country's governance, the aid and international optimism had largely dried up, deep fissures in the national political leadership and across the country had solidified and the nation's peace needed to be renewed afresh. Thankfully for the aspirations of rapid growth and development in the national economy, oil and gas monies flowing in from the Timor Sea meant a new tap could be turned on. By the second decade of the twenty-first century, the Timor-Leste government was intent on developing its own oil- and gas-led economy. The country was awash with the hope of prosperity.

***

In mid-2018, while passing through Dili, I received an invitation from a foreign diplomat to address her staff. She and I had met before when I addressed her in her home country about culture in Timor-Leste. She wanted me to offer a similar briefing to her program staff and associated donor organisations working in Timor-Leste. Some of their Timorese counterparts and staff would also be at the presentation.

Having been told I could not take a mobile phone or computer into the meeting room without prior security clearance, I arrived empty-handed at the compound. Given the high level of security, I was surprised by my low-key vetting by the Timorese staff. I announced in Tetum that I was there for a meeting and apologised for being 15 minutes early. They quickly looked for my name on the list and let me through. Another woman had also arrived early. 'Are you here for the meeting?' she asked when we had cleared security. 'Come on in.' We walked past a tall man, presumably the head of mission, who cheerily waved us through. The woman and I quickly found common ground and cause in our interest in all things Timor. Engrossed in our conversation, I was surprised when I looked up to see the time was well past the hour. The head of mission entered the room in a fluster. 'We are all here,' he assured the many people now gathered there. 'It's just that we are having a slight problem locating our speaker.'

After I had properly identified myself as the speaker, we went around the room introducing ourselves. Many of the foreigners in the room were eager to hear from me on how they might overcome what they termed the 'cultural barriers to development' in Timor. While some mentioned ideas around working with culture, others framed their problems in terms of Timorese culture and the barriers it created for their work. I began my presentation suggesting that many 'cultural barriers' may in fact emanate from the non-Timorese culture. There may be unexamined barriers to thinking through different understandings, even different realities. I suddenly felt nervous. I didn't want to offend the people I was here to engage. The woman I came in with looked across the table and smiled. She gave me a wink, letting me know it was okay with her. I relaxed a little.

The questions I received were diverse. They ranged from domestic violence, marriage exchange, land laws, agriculture and nutrition (and food taboos), economic surplus, cultural ceremonies, history and the post-conflict reinvigoration of tradition, post-conflict trauma and violence, health and healing (particularly for women), economic priorities and youth attitudes, ritual resource governance and the effects of such practices on conservation and community governance. My head was spinning.

The many Timorese staff of the various organisations in the room conveyed, in a variety of ways, their commitment to customary processes and exchanges, despite the real difficulties they pose. Quite a few noted their own partial resistance to some customary practices, mainly because of the ways they drain their own 'city-based' economic resources. Constant obligations to customary sets of relations are a burden on such Dili-based Timorese. Even if they don't always have to travel back to their districts or related communities for rituals, they are expected to send money home to assist in enabling the rituals and the transfer of goods. Yet even the most critical voices conveyed the necessity of their participation in such exchange processes. What was important, some said, was their obligation to honour their ancestors, no matter the difficulties for their individual livelihoods.

Such broad acceptance was a revelation for many of the foreigners in the room. Outsiders tend to hear the criticism of customary processes by Timorese people as a signal that they would prefer to abandon such practices. In this instance, the Timorese staff expressed an in-principle commitment to ritual and custom, despite the misgivings and hardships they might entail. This distinction is very important. At one point, one of the Timorese women remarked on how her rural parents attributed her success in life to their ongoing ritual sacrifices and honoured ancestral connections. This comment prompted much laughter around the room among the foreigners and the Timorese (including the storyteller herself). But their laughter was, I discerned, of a different order. One group was incredulous; the other group laughed in acknowledgement of the deep paradoxes and contradictions within which 'modern' Timorese live their lives.

In my many conversations with foreign aid and development workers in Timor-Leste, I have noticed that it is often within the agricultural sector that development workers struggle most, especially with the cultural aspects of Timorese livelihood practices. With their focus on efficiency and markets, foreigners will often remark on the travesty of wasted resources and priorities given by rural people to ceremonial life. They observe that people who are so poor and nutritionally challenged think nothing of slaughtering many of their livestock for rituals. All that good food, just wasted. They lament that Timorese rural people continue to feed their children poor-quality foods despite all the nutritional education that has been delivered. The Timorese are criticised for being slow to immerse themselves in the market economy. Another criticism is that Timorese have such large families and invest so greatly in marriage exchange. Some outsiders perceive that these priorities, along with what many consider to be futile ceremonies, are placed above children's health, wellbeing and education.

Other foreigners are more circumspect and reflexive. One woman from an international organisation told me once how over the four years she had been in Timor she had been introduced to customary practices very slowly. Reflecting back, she said that it felt like every six months or so her Timorese staff ramped up her exposure to 'cultural aspects' of their work. She noted that this was usually just when she had begun thinking that she understood Timorese ways of doing things. Her work helping to set up community conservation areas had been constantly challenging, not least because of the time each negotiation took. She said she was finally learning that if a section of the customary community was missing (if, say, individuals had moved from the community or fled to West Timor) then governance negotiations could not proceed until a way was found to ameliorate or address their absence. In such cases, communities needed time—and sometimes a lot of time—to figure out a way to make the absent party present, to enable processes to move forward so a governance arrangement could be negotiated and agreed. Problems, she had learnt, would also arise when people now living in a particular community were claiming or using land that was not customarily theirs. In these cases, complicated negotiations were needed to find a way to involve these people in governance relationships. These fraught and emotionally charged processes all took time, with people also needing space, and sometimes outside assistance, to negotiate a way forward.

My role at this briefing was awkward, as was my very presence as 'key speaker'. I was a foreigner being asked to speak to a bunch of other foreigners in the East Timorese capital about Timorese culture. Why had they asked me? Why had I accepted? Why, even as I made sure to give space for the Timorese present to respond to the questions posed, did I feel compelled to add other perspectives? It was not a role I relished, and I felt very uncomfortable. But I also felt like being this spokesperson was something that the many Timorese people I had lived and worked with over many years expected me to do.

Most Timorese people grow up learning that knowledge is partial, that your perspective depends on where you are from. They know, too, that rural Timorese norms and customs are different across the country; sometimes they are even different in the same village. They know, because they continually do it, that 'truths' about places and histories and cultures are worked out in the moment, in context, and in constant negotiation with others. Even so, given the chance, most Timorese will forcefully put forward their particular view of the world. Foreigners in Timor are inclined to be in search of facts and absolutes. Hence, when an individual Timorese speaks about 'their culture', these outsiders don't hear it as partial—they hear it as fact.

My work as an anthropologist and geographer forces me to pay attention to the partial truths and constant negotiations that make up people's lives. Because I am trained to think this way—to pay attention, listen, observe and unpack the nuance—I comfort myself in uncomfortable circumstances, like this donor briefing, that it is this 'academic rigour' that I can offer in such conversations. Of course, there are also Timorese anthropologists, such as Josh Trindade, an anthropologist and senior government adviser. For people like Josh, this cultural 'translator' role can also, I imagine, be uncomfortable. At international forums I have watched as he has carefully explained particular Timorese social and cultural histories and processes. Often, after such presentations, there will be someone in the audience (a foreigner or a Timorese) who will imply that he doesn't really understand something. For Timorese interlocutors, the concern is usually cultural ('this is not how my group see it/tell it/ do it'). For foreigners, the sentiments expressed are often 'anti-culture', implying that culture is being used as an excuse for poverty or inequality. Despite the challenges, Josh remains nonchalant: 'It's my job to try to explain these things,' he says. I would hazard to guess that it is also something he feels is his cultural duty.

* * *

As I set out above, much of my own partial understanding of Timorese life and lives comes about through the intimacies and confusions of life lived as an 'outsider' through the *longue durée*—life lived with my Timorese husband, extended family and friends working together, eating together, celebrating and mourning together. And sometimes fighting together. As I have come to know more about the richly interconnected worlds of Timorese cultural and ecological communities, I have also learnt about their life pathways. I have begun to see and, more importantly, feel the connections between people, their lands, waters, local histories, politics and associated rituals of life and death. As I have investigated these connections as an academic, people often explicitly ask me to record and take their stories to those in power. I have come to realise that people do not share their stories without reason; they expect me to weave something new with their knots and threads. As the cloth takes shape, so too do my obligations to these people and all their varied aspirations.

While I have written academic books and articles around these topics, here I tell a more personal story of chance encounters and brief anecdotes, of hunches gleaned and insights sharpened—often painfully so—during my many years carrying out research in the country and during the travels I made across the island with my young family in 2018. I have learnt, over the years, how it is often the quotidian or seemingly unremarkable stories that I stumble upon that lead, eventually, to the greatest understanding.

I have learnt about the need to give these stories and encounters time, and to take the time to tune in, to notice, to see, to hear and to feel things in often unaccustomed ways.

Throughout the book, I reflect on encounters and my own intimate and proximate relationships with a range of people: customary leaders, families, farmers, drivers, members of Timorese civil society movements, international development workers, university students and national political leaders. These encounters and the associated stories, beings and places reveal both the everyday politics and poetics of life on island Timor. While the book tracks a journey across the island, each chapter has its own specific and cross-cutting themes and, as such, can also be read on its own.

I begin this story with an opportunity we had to spend an extended period of time travelling through the country, and our arrival in the far west of the island. Although I had been travelling to Timor, often with Quin and our children, every year for more than a decade, I had not spent much time in Indonesian West Timor. Quin and our children had never been there. So, we decided to begin our six-month trip to the island by flying via Bali to the Indonesian provincial capital of Kupang. Through encounters in the capital and rural areas, cross-island cultural similarities and differences are thrown into relief. Whether they be refugees from Timor-Leste's 'independence vote' or ordinary West Timorese, a variety of perspectives underscore how lives on the Indonesian side of the border are entwined with historical and contemporary events in Timor-Leste. In Chapter 2, a visit to Timor-Leste's exclave of Oecusse draws out the everyday challenges of post-conflict rebuilding and economic development. According to many local people, customary processes are being sidelined in the government's rush to showcase the development possibilities for this enclave. The question is, at what political cost?

Chapter 3 reflects on the history of movements across a long-contested border and the ways in which local people's awareness of their shared history and culture is shaped by their complex personal circumstances. Through personal stories and encounters, we can glean the reasons why people choose to settle on either side of this new international border. In Chapter 4, in a village straddling Indonesia and Timor-Leste, we explore the ways Timor's migratory wild honey bees challenge the division of colonial borders that have long separated people, places and histories in the region. With bees understood to be spirit people, their travels and honey are shown to be essential to the material and spiritual unity of life for border peoples.

Heading to Dili, in Chapter 5, our gaze shifts to the politics of *lulik* (ancestral potency, sacred, forbidden, taboo) and the ways in which politics in Timor-Leste is as much about ancestral pathways as it is about democracy. Both processes involve deep understandings of power. Reflecting on a national election campaign, we trace the way in which an ancestral politics is made visible, plays out and becomes legitimised. In Chapter 6, a journey from Dili to the smaller island of Atauro involves encounters with island residents that draw out the ways in which centuries-long migrations across the region are encoded in the landscape and made present today. The challenges of re-establishing connections to the past and among people are illuminated in unexpected ways.

Arriving in Quin's hometown of Baucau in the east of the island, Chapter 7 focuses on the ways in which cultural life in this region is organised around the flow of water. These above- and below-ground flows bind together and course through the veins of both people and their landscape. Some worry that a proposed industrial development might threaten these flows. This question, they say, will be answered by the response of the ancestral realm. Likewise, Chapter 8 examines how illness and healing are understood through the consubstantiated relationship between people, their environments and their ancestors. Following the healing journey of a young man and his extended family through a spring-based ritual, we see the interwoven nature of these relations and the ways in which these practices underpin understandings of health and cultural identity. Continuing on with this theme, Chapter 9 traces everyday life during the rice harvest season in the village of Bercoli, showing it to be richly punctuated by hard work and play, ritual and proscription. What you can and cannot do is a matter of continual negotiation and anticipation between people and the spirit realm. It is a life with its own complex rhythms and, despite the challenges, a shared commitment to living together well.

Chapter 10 provides insights into what happens when you take 20 Australian university students on a study tour of this complex land. How do they and their hosts respond? Leading this field class is an annual role that I have, sometimes reluctantly, taken on as a way of bringing foreigners (my own students) into the ambit and intrigue of Timor-Leste and its citizenry's lives. What relations and understandings can be forged and negotiated in these often-unsettling spaces? In Chapter 11, continuing the theme of unsettling spaces, we learn how rights to land, especially women's rights to land, is a major issue in post-conflict Timor-Leste and the subject of critical debate. In little-recognised counter-narratives, rural people subtly speak back to these debates from their own historical and cultural circumstances. Their commentary and practices elucidate the perverse effects of a development agenda that seeks to supersede rather than work with local lives and priorities. In Chapter 12, we also explore the ways in which, in Timor's rural areas, people are frequently preoccupied with the past. Addressing the past is the only way, they say, that they can live well in the present and ensure the wellbeing of future generations. Culminating in highly organised and affective performances of cultural capacity, these ritual practices are vital in enabling healing at multiple levels and time periods.

In the final chapter and the subsequent epilogue, we draw some conclusions around the ideas and practices of living well in a house-based society. House building brings people together and enables relations to begin and, in some cases, to be concluded. For my own family, house building is a statement of reconnection to a place and its people. In an increasingly volatile global context, the future of this reconnection is both comforting and uncertain.

* * *

The themes that shape this book and my own thinking about Timor-Leste emerge through this journey from west to east, from the outside of Timor-Leste into its rural heart and back out again. These recursive movements from the outside in are also the movements and structures that organise Timorese cultural life. Josh Trindade often talks about Timorese culture as having an inner realm and an outer realm. At the heart of the inner realm lies the concept of *lulik*, which can be at once an idea, an object, a being, a place, a phenomenon, a word or a practice. While *lulik*, as Josh says, is the core orienting principle of Timorese lives, for foreigners, little of this is immediately apparent. Rather, visitors to the country—usually development workers, business people, diplomats and their associates—are exposed and familiarised in the first instance to an outer, more public realm, one dominated by the secular concerns of politics, development and the formal economy. Yet, for Timorese themselves, even this outer realm is intimately linked to the inner realm of *lulik* and their own intensely networked ancestral, historical and interpersonal concerns.

This book is about spiralling down through these layers to find a country and its people redolent in the capacity to accommodate and value both of these life realms. It is an enticement to others to encounter the island and nourish their own curiosity for, and relationships to, the land, its people and its spirit.

1

The Not-So-Wild West

As we were landing in Kupang, I noticed that something was strange on this side of the island. At first, I couldn't put my finger on the difference. Later I realised it was the sheer orderliness of the place. The straight lines, neat rows of houses and relative civic order were completely unlike what I was used to by now in Timor-Leste. On our descent into El Tari International Airport, I had glimpsed an area outside town with rows of encampment-style housing. Was that where the East Timorese had lived, I wondered? I tried to remember the names and locations of the camps in Kupang where thousands of East Timorese forced to flee East Timor in 1999 had been relocated by the Indonesian army.

Kupang, not unlike Dili, was a ramshackle, hot and dusty 'Wild West'–styled trading port. A relic of the Dutch era, it is located at the western tip of island Timor. Despite its involvement in periodic local resource booms (manganese mining being the most recent), it still found itself the capital of one of Indonesia's poorest provinces, Nusa Tengara Timur. For us, Kupang was also a convenient starting point for our plans to participate in a traditional honey harvest ceremony, a highly orchestrated event that would take place in the border regions in the middle of the island. A friend from there, Agus, was picking us up at the airport.

At the time of my first visit in 2011, my academic colleague (and Agus's brother) Balthasar and I had been researching Timorese people's connections with freshwater springs. Visiting their extended family from the border kingdom of Lookeu, I had gleaned deep insight into the ways in which water and springs had, much like this Lookeu family, moved for centuries back and forth across eastern and western parts of the island.

The colonial-imposed border divided not only the island but also its people, including the people of the traditional mountainous kingdom of Lookeu, the royal domain of Agus and Balthasar's ancestors.

Photo 3: Rice fields and mountains in the kingdom of Lookeu.

Awaiting my return flight back to Australia, I was languishing in the tropical heat of one of Kupang airport's outdoor eateries. After a physically and emotionally intense visit, I was pleased with the research and happy to be returning home to my family. To pass the time, Agus began telling me intriguing stories about bees and wild honey harvests, of ceremonies involving whole communities and of his own ability to morph into the role of a *laku* during these events.

Laku, in the Tetum Terik language of the border region, refers to the Asian palm civet cat. However, as I learnt in the case of the honey harvest, *laku* refers to a specific group of men who, at certain times of the year, take on the persona of a *laku* and climb tens of metres into the forest canopy in pursuit of wild honey, bee larvae and wax. Like the civet cat, these men only climb in the darkness of the night. Like the cats, they call out to each other and to others around as they search out the sweetness hidden within the canopy's branches. Brave and sonorous, these human *laku* climb great heights comfortably to secure honey and wax accompanied only by firesticks, smoke and song. Once in the canopy, they silently receive the inevitable stings on their scantily clad bodies, while imploring the bees to descend and give up their 'houses' (hives) for the benefit of those gathered below to sing, dance and consume the honey and bee larvae. Agus had once been a *laku* himself. Listening to his stories, I knew that this would not be my only visit. In retrospect, I think that Agus was already hooking me in.

Balthasar is a family friend and a long-term academic collaborator. Born in Portuguese Timor, 'the hands of destiny' (in his own words) led him to attend formal education in West Timor and Flores, Indonesia, and in different parts of the world. In 1993, he was awarded a doctoral degree in philosophy by Columbia University in New York. In his later life he decided to refocus his attention away from Western philosophy and return to the indigenous philosophies he had lived during his youth. In appearance and demeanour, the two brothers are strikingly different. Balthasar is lean with fine angular features, while Agus has much broader facial features and a more muscular physique. The latter is something of a raconteur and adventurer with a keen ear for a story and an eye for logistics. A university technical administrator, he had spent many years in his youth working as the offsider for the Darwin-based historian Peter Spillett. Together they travelled the island, sourcing and carrying out interviews with customary elders about Timor's precolonial history. Agus, like his five other brothers, was also deeply versed in tradition and had always been keen to resume this role of cultural brokerage.

So, in April 2018, I arrived back in Kupang, this time with my husband, Quin, and our two children, Madalena and Zeca, then aged 8 and 11. Agus had meticulously organised the details of our visit, all the while trying to allay concerns that the honey harvest was still some way off—if indeed it was to happen at all. '*Wani sedauk tama*,' he told me, somewhat anxiously. ('The bees have not entered.') Just what the bees were still to enter, I was not yet sure. In the meantime, we had some time on our hands.

At Quin's instigation, we visited the Chinese temple down in the old port area. To get there we had to find our way through the old part of town. We spent a brief but intense period of time hustling ourselves and the kids through the frenetic traffic of motorbikes and brightly coloured minibuses, music blaring. Kupang was not a place for walkers. Yet, in the narrow streets of this part of town, there was still a scattering of old Dutch and Chinese colonial architecture. Its close and bustling atmosphere was also a reprieve from the more obnoxiously modern hotels and shopping malls springing up elsewhere.

Finally, we arrived at the temple. It had been built, we found out, in the mid-1800s by the then flourishing southern Chinese community, although it was later partially destroyed by aerial bombing in World War II. Its rebuilt frontage was still reminiscent of a traditional Chinese style, with impressive pillars and arch emblazoned with Chinese lettering and three concrete sculptures: crab, peacock and lizard. These, we were informed, represented the animals associated with the Chinese clans who had first established the temple using main pillars brought from mainland China. Quin's particular interest in visiting the temple was because he suspected that Kupang was the port of arrival for his paternal grandfather who had migrated from southern China via Macau and settled in the east of the island sometime around the 1900s.

The Timorese-Chinese caretakers of the temple greeted us warmly. They gave our kids cool drinks and brought out their holiday snaps from a past visit with some of their relatives in Sydney. Quin, too, has many relatives in Sydney; it was there that he had first found refuge in Australia in the mid-1990s. On this occasion though, try as they might, neither Quin nor the temple caretakers could establish direct connections between their respective Chinese families. Sydney was, for the moment at least, too far away. Neither did they know anything about his Chinese grandfather's arrival in Timor. They did, though, appreciate our visit.

We had planned to stay a while in the capital, but in the end, we didn't stay long. The heat that April was oppressive. On our second day, as we sought out lunch at an empty harbourside eatery, we asked the restaurateur where everyone was. 'The people in Kupang are like bats,' she exclaimed. 'They only come out at night.' Later, when we met Balthasar's sister-in-law who lives on the border, she said that Kupang is different to the rest of West Timor. When I asked how, she replied: 'Its sweaty heat makes your skin white.' It was not exactly the explanation I had been expecting. But, considering the restaurateur's comment, I guess it made sense.

As we left Kupang for Kefa, our next destination, we stopped at a shop on the urban fringe to buy some credit for our phones. Apart from Agus and his family, we hadn't met any East Timorese people since our arrival. Yet, here on the edge of town, in the heart of a bustling commercial hub, we found ourselves engaged in commerce with two young East Timorese women. The pair had fled the violence of their birthplace as small children. Now adult, they were yet to return to Timor-Leste. 'Our mothers, aunts and grandmothers go back now and then,' they said, adding nonchalantly: 'Our home is here. We live here among the locals. We are now local.'

For Quin, this was a revelation. To hear that these young women might not countenance a return was a little shocking to him. He, too, had been forced to flee his birth country. But, as soon as he was able, he had returned—at least for regular visits. 'What's stopping you from going back?' he asked incredulously. 'You are Timorese!' (clearly forgetting for a moment that he was actually in Timor). Perhaps by way of drawing them back into that shared identity, as we left Quin gave them each a little money and told them to study hard and not marry early. They were pleased, and I think a little touched by the gesture. There was in that exchange something unspoken between the three of them, something that drew them together, just as other factors held them apart. These are the interwoven connections between East Timorese that I have borne witness to on countless occasions: bonds forged through uneven mixtures of belonging, connection, displacement, unspeakable horror, joy, pride and determination.

As our journey east followed the increasingly rural roads, our driver Patrice pointed out the fertile and productive rice and vegetable fields along the way. 'These are all farmed by refugees from East Timor,' he said. 'They are such hard workers. Not like the locals, who are lazy.' It was the same refrain one hears about Indonesian workers in Timor-Leste, but in reverse. The newcomers to an area, Timorese say, always have to work harder. They don't have the land or family connections that locals can rely on to get by. Patrice was himself a quiet, hardworking young man. His wife and new baby were back on the border where Patrice usually worked as a truck driver for one of Balthasar's brothers. His parents were also refugees from further east, settling on the Indonesian side of the border after they fled the civil strife in Portuguese Timor in the 1970s.

Our drive to Kefa, where another of the Lookeu brothers lived, was on a relatively smooth but windy road. It struck me, again, that the houses and gardens we passed along the way were so much more orderly than was typical of Timor-Leste. Absent, too, were the waving throngs of children that, in Timor-Leste, are a constant in every village you pass through. These villages seemed to be largely deserted. People are busy, I was told; they are all out working. It was notable that even the most modern of houses had a round open-sided hut alongside it, many with a tin rather than traditional thatched roof. These day huts were the household-level custom houses of the region, places where family 'business' gets done, and where corn and other goods are stored. Similar, but more enclosed and elaborate, clan-level origin houses could also be glimpsed from time to time. Ancestral traditions, it was evident, were even here still redolent in everyday life.

Everywhere we travelled, there were roadside billboards featuring candidates in the forthcoming provincial elections. Chatting to the people we met along the way, politics seemed to be on everyone's lips. Many, it seemed, were hoping for the election of a Timorese-born governor. Since El Tari, the popular and respected Timorese-born governor (1966–78), the majority of the governors have come from the neighbouring island of Flores, and an increasingly large Florenese population now dominates Kupang's political, administrative and business life. Some people muttered that they would like West Timor to become a separate province, if the right leader should emerge. By this, they meant someone smart, capable and, above all, someone who has 'people' or a large support base. In the forthcoming elections, there were three main contenders: the first-ever female candidate from the island of Rote, a Catholic candidate from Flores and a Protestant candidate from Timor.

West Timor is often characterised as half Catholic and half Protestant (with the latter mainly living in the far west). Some people spoke to us about how their half-island population was changing. They spoke in hushed tones of an unofficial internal migration program that actively encouraged many devout Muslim Indonesians to settle on the island, especially along the border. Lands, too, they said, were increasingly being bought up by outsiders. In these areas, people talked worriedly about their perceptions of an increasing Islamisation of the region and of the rapid pace at which mosques were being built. They mentioned the ever-increasing number of Javanese and Sumatran restaurants and furniture-making businesses lining the roadsides of West Timor's major towns. They said that forests were increasingly being logged and used to make furniture for export to Timor-Leste, a nation they now associated with American dollars and wealth.

Through all our encounters and conversations, it was not yet clear to me what people in West Timor made of Timor-Leste's independence and new nation status. Was there hostility about its decision to separate from the Indonesian state, ambivalence about its status, or pride and hope founded on a common Timorese identity? I thought I discerned a mixture of all three, but these reactions were not something people spoke openly about.

***

The next stop in our journey was Kefamenanu (Kefa), a forlorn market town nestled in the plateau of several mountain ranges. There we planned to spend time with Niko, another of Balthasar's brothers, and his wife, Effie. Niko, born into a royal house across the border in Fatumean, was now a local high school principal. Effie, herself a descendant of local Kefa royalty, was a district bureaucrat. Both, we found out, continued to practice their ancestral house-based religions at the same time as being devout Catholics. One day they took us to their church. A newly built, monumental brick structure of cavernous proportions, it stood alone in its remote rural landscape. Its stark architectural emptiness was more than matched though by the raucous beauty of the many local school children singing and marching in the church grounds as they practised for the events of a forthcoming saint's day. The local priest came over to greet us warmly, exceedingly happy at a rare foreign visit.

Later in the car, I asked Effie about how marriage relations played out in this part of the country. I was curious to know if it was like Timor-Leste where the marital alliances between couples and their associated origin houses are cemented through the exchange of cultural goods. 'Oh yes,' she said, 'it's still strong.' This surprised me, perhaps because adherence to these practices seemed at odds with the veneer of modernity we could see everywhere in this part of the country, including the many large buildings and monuments celebrating the state and organised religion. Effie explained that intermarrying families still actively exchange cattle, money and goats. Pigs are also exchanged, but they are used more for feasting. The particular details of the exchange would, she said, depend on the customs of the intermarrying origin houses, the socioeconomic status of the families and, very often, the educational level of the couple. Effie told me that in one part of Flores, where her father was from, the 'price' is raised for every level of education the woman had completed.

Niko and Effie had met at university, but in many ways their marriage had followed an ancient path of alliance-making. Building on a long-standing alliance between the respective houses, Niko's family from Fatumean had brought buffalo across the border to the palace of Biboki in Tam Kesi, Effie's birthplace. The name Tam Kesi is derived from Tetum Terik words meaning to enter and become tied/bound to place (*tama*=to enter, *kesi*=to tie). We decided that while in Kefa we would make a visit to the Tam Kesi palace. It was to be the first time that Effie had returned since she was eight years old.

Photo 4: View from Biboki highlands towards Oecusse.

It was a two-hour trip from Kefa to the palace. Without local knowledge, we would have had no hope of finding it. What started as a narrow road as we wound through the villages of the Biboki kingdom then became a dirt path across high grasslands filled with herds of cattle and horses. From these green pastures we could see all the way to Timor-Leste, both the mountainous ring to the north-west that enclosed the drylands of the coastal exclave of Oecusse and the forested mountains of Fatumean in Suai much further to the east. After passing through a 'gate' marked by a thicket of trees, we descended slightly to the base of two karstic megaliths that now blocked our path. Niko and Effie stopped the vehicles in the thickly forested grove and set off by foot down to the local village to seek permission to enter the palace. They returned with the village head's wife who led us through the forest and an opening in a low rock fence. From there, we entered an exquisite assembly of houses set among elaborate stone terracing. Passing through an area dedicated to ornately carved ritual poles, we were flanked on our right by the megaliths, and on our left by the stone walls and steps leading up a steep hill through terraced earthen courtyards and rock altars. The latter belonged, respectively, to six large, round wooden origin houses, all with thatched roofing. A small group of women were gathered under the roof of the first house. One was weaving cloth; others were chatting beside a pile of drying wild tubers that were to be onsold to Chinese merchants for use in the cosmetic industry.

We headed up the steps that wound past the five subsidiary origin houses until we reached the main house of the king. The king was out, tending his animals. A young girl was given some money to go and fetch him by motorbike taxi. It seemed that visiting in the company of descended royalty gave us certain privileges.

When he finally arrived, the king's visual appearance was little different to any other farmer we had passed along the way. What he lacked in majestic visual impact, though, he made up for in oratory ability. He carefully explained to us the importance of this setting for local lives and the wider governance of the Timor Tengah Utara (TTU) district for which Kefa is the capital. The palace complex housed six families, although many more lived in the village below. The twinned megaliths, understood as a cosmological pairing of male and female complementarity, were the centre of their religious life. In times of communal hardship, such as drought or famine, the villagers would come together to sacrifice a goat and a rooster on the peaks. Both animals would be carried alive along a treacherous path to the top of the 'male' megalith. It was almost impossible to see where people could ascend these sheer rock faces, but apparently they could do so with a goat strung across the shoulders and a chicken tucked under the arm. The goat would be killed and eaten atop the megalith. The rooster would be tied to the top and left there, crowing until it died. The ritual was to serve as redress for any community wrongdoing and to encourage the ancestral spirits to return to the people their livelihood, fertility and the rains.

Later, the king elaborated on the connections between the palace of Tam Kesi and other places across island Timor. 'This is one of the most powerful sites in the whole region,' he said. Every new governor of the TTU district would come to Tam Kesi prior to taking office. There the governor would make an offering and receive in return the sacred governing power emanating from the palace. Indeed, the king told us, Tam Kesi is the origin centre of island Timor, the place from where all the other kingdoms spread. Its daughters, he said, continue to marry out into these kingdoms, including into Timor-Leste and the royal houses of Oecusse and Fatumean. Here, again, it was clear that beneath the veneer of order and modernity, West and East Timor have as much in common customarily as that which currently divides them politically.

Photo 5: The main palace at Tam Kesi.

Photo 6: Honeycomb in the megaliths of Tam Kesi.

As we spoke with the king among the rock altars, houses and megaliths of the palace, he was careful to instruct us where we could and couldn't photograph according to the potency of each site. Our children and Niko and Effie's children ('town kids') played ball in the courtyard of the main house. Towards the end of our discussions, I looked over and saw to my horror that they were resting the ball precariously on a rock altar in front of the main house. I imagined my son rushing in to kick it off at any moment. The king was seemingly unfazed by the incident, but it took me some time to recover. Nonetheless, at the end of our visit, he called the children over and blessed them by sprinkling water over them and blowing on the crowns of their heads. They were now safe to return home.

Our descent from the place wound a loop around the rear of the twin megaliths. From there, the mountains of Timor-Leste felt close enough to reach out and touch. It was then that I noticed a gigantic honeycomb drooping dramatically down a cliff edge halfway up the male megalith. A good sign, I thought to myself. In Tam Kesi, the bees had already entered.

·

2

Enclave Society

Quin and the kids were travelling on East Timorese passports, so they could easily cross by land into the Oecusse exclave of Timor-Leste. But, for me, it was not so straightforward. When I finally received notification that I had secured a visa, we were off. From Kefa, the border was an hour or so drive up a steep mountainous climb. On the way, we passed through the village of Napan. This place was full of pro-Indonesian militia in 1999, our driver Patrice told us.

We reached the tiny mountain border post and began the seemingly endless checks required by the full gamut of bureaucracies housed on the hillside. First, we presented ourselves to the Indonesian military, then to the Indonesian police, then the health department, immigration and customs. At each checkpoint, our passports were intently scrutinised. Eventually our names would be logged in a book and we would be sent on to the next tiny house.

Quin talked incessantly with each officer we met. I could tell he was nervous. Back in 1994 when he was a student in Indonesia, he had helped to organise an East Timorese resistance protest during the Asia-Pacific Economic Cooperation summit in Jakarta. United States President Bill Clinton was to be an attendee, so it was a prime opportunity to garner media attention for the Timorese cause. During the protest, Quin was arrested and then interrogated by Indonesian intelligence for two weeks. He was finally released due to international pressure, and the East Timorese student resistance network organised for him to flee to Australia through the backdoor of the Balinese airport. The Timorese stationed there as custom officers had literally driven him out onto the tarmac.

For Quin, like most Timorese, checkpoints and immigration processes reignite the memories of such traumatic times, particularly when the authorities are Indonesian.

Yet that day, as usual, those nerves were hidden behind a jovial deference that he was extending to his country's former occupiers. He talked nonstop about anything he thought might break the ice, cut through formalities and make a connection: his children, his travels, his knowledge of particular people or places in Indonesia. At one stage, the kids and I were asked to go pose in the middle of the border for a photo with one of the Indonesian guards. At long last, we made it through.

The Indonesian border guards, by now friendly, even broke their own rules and let us drive our car through to the East Timorese border post a kilometre away on the other side. From there, another car was waiting to take us to the Oecusse capital, Pante Makasar. On this day, the 1 km drive through no-man's-land was desolate, but we were told that once a month it transformed into a lively marketplace where locals from both sides of the border came to sell their goods.

Once we arrived at the small bamboo shack that constituted the East Timorese military checkpoint, the atmosphere was immediately more relaxed. Nonetheless, the customs officer asked us to place our bags on his desk for inspection. As the desk heaved and nearly broke under the weight of our suitcase, he promptly abandoned the task. Despite the hundreds of millions of dollars currently being poured by the Timorese government into Oecusse's new special economic zone, known as ZEESM, the proper fitting-out of mountain border posts was clearly not yet a priority.

After clearing customs, we loaded our bags into our changeover car, farewelled Patrice and waited while our new driver hitched a lift back across the border to buy some cheap cigarettes. The man who escorted him across was an Indonesian military officer. Quin enjoyed the chance to banter with the Timorese border guards about local politics and happenings. In contrast to the deference he had just shown to the Indonesian authorities, now he was talking so casually he could have been with his own family.

As we piled into the car and headed down the mountains towards the coast and Pante Makasar, we could all sense the change in the place, both physically and emotionally. The road was immediately terrible, made of dirt and badly potholed. There were many small thatched origin houses, and everywhere people and children waving to us. Almost immediately, our driver began to point out landmarks. With still raw emotion, he gestured to various sites along the way where, in 1999, Timorese attempting to flee the militia violence had been massacred. He pointed out the places where they were beaten, where they were killed and where they were thrown off a cliff. Private memorials dotted the hillside. We knew for sure we were back in Timor-Leste. He said we were not far from the village of Passabe, the site of a massacre by pro-Indonesian militias in the wake of the 1999 referendum.

Our new driver, a 30-something, self-assured man called Manuel, was born in the east, near Quin's own hometown of Baucau. The Makasae-speaking people from Baucau are known to be tough (it was these people that Patrice had referred to as hardworking refugees earlier in our journey). Manuel's mother was a Baikeno-speaking woman from Oecusse and he had grown up there. He told us how, before the militias left East Timorese in 1999, they had flooded into Oecusse. In a murderous fury they had forced most of the population to flee to the mountains inside Indonesia. They burnt nearly everything to the ground, even the toilets. They shot the livestock and felled the forests of teak, taking the spoils with them as they withdrew.

As we descended further into the valley, we saw groups of people in the fields harvesting their rice. I asked Manuel to stop just as we reached the valley floor, so I could take a photo of a cluster of origin houses. They reminded me of smaller versions of the origin houses I had seen a few years before in the mountains of Lookeu and Fatumean in Timor-Leste. We chatted with the people mingling outside and remarked on this similarity. A man joined us and told us that his younger brother married a woman from Fatumean. Indeed, a delegation of his family had made the journey across two international borders to negotiate the marriage exchange. As is so very often the case, it didn't take long to find a connection. This woman from Fatumean turned out to be Balthasar's niece, Adelina, whose mother was from Lookeu in West Timor. Many of her family lived in Lookeu, our destination, after Oecusse, for the honey harvest. Adelina had studied in Australia where she had shared a house with Balthasar in a street very close to our own home.

Here in Oecusse, Adelina's husband's family told us that the people in Fatumean customarily ask for buffalo from the origin house into which their daughter is marrying. But, as many local houses no longer have buffalo, they took *morten* (red coral bead necklace) and money instead. Surprised and pleased with this unexpectedly close encounter on our first hour in Oecusse, we arranged a return visit to learn more about life in the nearby foothills. We were told to bring with us betel nut and leaf, candles and a rooster.

***

Manuel was a passionate supporter of the ZEESM special economic zone project that had been underway in the Oecusse-Ambeno Territory for a number of years. He was also an active militant of the youth wing of the FRETILIN political party, the party that had carriage of the ZEESM project. He had been involved in several construction projects, including a shiny new basketball and outdoor recreation facility. As we drove through the valley, he told us how ZEESM was transforming Oecusse. 'There are now so many jobs and so much development,' he enthused. 'Soon people in Oecusse will not have to grow corn or rice. They will have enough money to buy their food.' Escaping life as a rural farmer is an idea that resonates with many Timorese ideas about prosperity and the future. The last thing most people want their children to be is a farmer. Modernity is characterised for these people as the pathway 'out of the darkness' of rural life and into 'the light' of the future.

We passed a new irrigation dam, at which point the potholed dirt road, which would be impassable in the wet season, abruptly ended. We were now in ZEESM territory. A slick, wide bitumen road led from there into the town. Along the way, we saw large groups of people gathered in their newly irrigated rice fields. Some were harvesting rice; others were loading it into trucks parked along the roadside. Apart from the trucks, there was not much traffic on the road. Most rural people in Oecusse do not have motorbikes, let alone cars. Instead, their pigs and goats and cattle congregated on the bitumen, and the dogs clearly enjoyed sleeping upon its warm surface.

With the national election in Timor-Leste less than a month away, many political party flags were flying outside the houses as we drove by. Many of these flags were grouped closely together, sometimes even when they represented opposing parties. Manuel told us that this election had split families along party lines. 'Especially in the mountains,' he said, 'if brothers fly different flags they will stop talking to each other. They will exclude each other from weddings and parties.' 'Understandings of democracy here have a way to go,' he mused.

Manuel predicted that the FRETILIN party, who also formed the incumbent Timor-Leste government, would win Oecusse in a landslide. 'They have produced results,' he said. 'People want development, not incessant talk about the past—which is all the other parties are offering.' He was annoyed by the other parties' preoccupation with the political history of the resistance struggle and who was the nation's biggest hero. 'In any case,' he said, 'the answer is clear. FRETILIN is the party of the resistance.'

All over Oecusse we encountered large billboards featuring the prime minister and architect of the ZEESM project, Dr Mari Alkatiri. The text on each billboard varied, but on each he was depicted staring off into the distance with a satisfied smile, and all highlighted the good and ongoing works of Dr Mari and his ZEESM team. Billboards for the pro-development FRETILIN political party also dotted the landscape. *Oras to'o ona* ('The time has come'), they proclaimed. The main FRETILIN campaign rally for Oecusse was scheduled for a week's time. 'Then,' declared Manuel, 'the mountain villages will empty out as everyone descends to Oecusse town to show their support for Mari and ZEESM.'

The town centre featured even wider newly paved roads and footpaths. Shiny new ZEESM administrative buildings, an international medical clinic, a new airport and a large resort hotel were all under various stages of construction. International flights would be starting soon, we were told. Oecusse was going to become the world's transit point into Timor-Leste.

On the day we arrived, however, the town was disconcertingly empty. We were told that was because people in Oecusse mainly now worked at night as labourers and were asleep during the day. But that night the town remained largely devoid of people, even along the town's picturesque waterfront where we went to dine. A small group of Portuguese engineers and assorted other foreigners were congregated in a Portuguese- and Spanish-run restaurant. The European football league blared from a large TV. A few Timorese patrons sat on plastic chairs across the road at the beach. These were the only signs of life on the waterfront.

Quin turned up late to meet us for dinner. He had been out for a walk, and further down the beach had encountered a local fisherman who had sought his help to haul in a bumper catch. The late afternoon rains and the resulting calm of the sea had created a windfall of fish. Ironically, the only fish on the menu in the restaurant came from New Zealand or Portugal. We had pizza, much to the delight of Madalena and Zeca.

The deserted city streets were transformed at dawn. Throngs of fluorescent-uniformed street cleaners descended on the wide streets and pavements to ensure the freshly minted orderliness remained intact. Then, by 9 am, the streets were empty again. As the heat set in, Quin and I realised we were exhausted from the journey so far and decided to rest at the motel. The kids were bored. The Timorese-Chinese owners of the motel had similar-aged children who had frequently been to Australia to visit their relatives. But even their international credentials and limited English were not enough to break the ice with Madalena and Zeca, who were always terribly shy with unfamiliar children. They sat around and moped. Suddenly, a piglet ran by the front door of our motel room. Zeca followed it and disappeared. So did Madalena. Later I found them gathered with the motel owner's children around a mother dog. She was suckling her young—only not all of them were puppies. One was the piglet! 'Its mother rejected it,' said the motel kids, 'and it wandered across the fields over to our place a while back.' The mother dog had taken it in.

This discovery was blissful for Zeca. Half 'wolf-boy', wherever he goes in Timor he always engrosses himself with the communities of dogs he encounters. He frequently relays to me his findings about particular dogs, their quirks and interrelationships. If the dogs don't already have names, he will give them one. Boss Dog, Mummy, The Dog Who Is Out of His Mind, Siak (Fierce) and a shy dog called Eng are the names he has bestowed on some of his long-term favourites in Baucau. (Eng was so-named because he heard the other kids frequently calling out '*Eng!*' to the dog and thought that was its name. He later found out *eng* means 'come' in the local Waima'a language. But the name stuck.) As his name suggests, Boss Dog was far less shy than Eng. Once he followed us to Sunday mass and refused to leave my feet the entire time. It was my first (and only) visit to that church and I only had the kids and their cousins with me. I can only guess what the villagers were saying about this strange foreigner who had brought her dog to mass.

Photo 7: Zeca and puppy with friends in the rice fields.

Dogs in Timor live freely. Their life is tough and often short, but it is full of adventure. At night, while people sleep, the dogs pay house calls on each other. When a female dog is in heat, the house of that dog will be packed day and night with brash canine visitors. These visits are lively affairs, and the associated pack fights and injuries are somewhat traumatising for Zeca who is always hanging around the edges of the pack. The positive side of these encounters, though, is new puppies—endless puppies and generation upon generation of family relationships for him to account for and reckon with. In Bercoli, the Baucau village where we often live, Mummy is the matriarch.

Sometimes I feel the need to shield the kids from the harsher human side of a Timorese dog's often short life. Dogs, especially puppies, are used as sacrifices in harvest rituals. Sometimes they will end up as a celebratory meal for a group of men after a hard day's work. One of Zeca's uncles likes nothing more than an impromptu meal whenever one of the household puppies is run over. Many dogs will die as a result of road accidents, others from injuries sustained when they steal meat from ritual preparations or attack machete-wielding farmers passing by the house.

Conversely, dogs in Timor have always made fieldwork much easier. Even in the most remote areas, the kids will usually find a puppy somewhere to play with (or else a piglet or one of the other countless domesticated baby animals running around). Telling people stories about the way Australians live with and care for their dogs is also another useful way to amuse people and pass the time, especially during the rice harvest season. People will be enthralled by these stories. Just the idea of having hospitals for dogs is enough to set them off into peals of laughter. Quin's favourite story to relay to his relatives involves canned dog food and the Timorese refugees who, recently arrived in Australia, were said to have bought dog food thinking it was a conveniently packaged meal—dogs on-demand available in all shapes and sizes. For Timorese people, piglets wandering into houses and becoming members of a canine family unit do not even touch the sides of strange. Back in Oecusse, Zeca and Madalena spent the day getting to know this multi-species family.

Towards dusk that evening, Manuel took us out to the new bridge to the west of town, another coveted symbol of the incoming 'light' of modernity. 'That's where the nightlife is really found,' he said. 'It's *rame* [lively].' This expensive and expansive bridge had been constructed over the mouth of the same river that, upstream, contained ZEESM's irrigation dam. The paved road, however, abruptly ended on the western side of the bridge. From there it was a long and bumpy slog along the coastal dirt road to the enclave's western border with Indonesia. From Manuel's description, I had been expecting riverside bars or eateries. Instead, there were a few trucks pulled over on the side of the bridge. The drivers of the trucks and some other youth on motorbikes were busily taking selfies with the bridge structure in the background. In sleepy Oecusse, this is what constituted nightlife.

Photo 8: Noefefan Bridge, Oecusse.

Prior to the bridge visit, Manuel had driven us to a site commemorating the first Portuguese landing on the island in Lifau in 1515. In 2015, the government had erected a large-scale memorial there. According to a speech by Timor-Leste's resistance hero and former prime minister Kay Rala Xanana Gusmao, the memorial was part of a celebration of the arrival of the Portuguese to the island. The memorial also commemorated the subsequent spread of the 'light' across eastern Timor. The 'light' was an implied reference to Christianity. Yet what was also implicit in his speech was a celebration of ZEESM and the spread of the light of modernity. Unlike the largely secular states of the West, the church and modernity are still synonymous in Timor-Leste.

At the site, a large bronze replica of a Portuguese ship and its various learned crew had been installed on the foreshore. These foreign men were depicted greeting the customary chiefs of Oecusse who were there presumably to extend their welcome. Although only a few years old, the memorial was already crumbling in places. Manuel attributed the shoddy appearance to a last-minute rush to have the memorial ready in time for the 500-year anniversary celebration. It was also, he said, a clear example of how the Xanana's political party, CNRT, could not be depended upon to get things done properly—unlike FRETILIN.

Photo 9: Monument to the Portuguese arrival, Lifau.

During our visit, a police guard emerged from a building and asked us to sign the visitors' book. Aside from bands of street sweepers (the same ones we had seen at dawn in the town), we were the only visitors at the site. We chatted with the street sweepers who had looked a little forlorn as they swept up fallen flowers from the deserted grounds. But they were cheery enough, now donning impressive broadbrimmed project-issue hats to keep off the sun. In Oecusse, street sweeping is a full-time job. They told us that they sweep from 6 am to 6 pm. There were a couple of hundred people in total, earning the minimum wage of US$115 per month, a substantial sum in Oecusse.

Back at the motel, we met Jose, a project manager from the ZEESM construction project and a friend of Manuel. He, too, was from the east, but had married a woman from Oecusse. She, like him, was descended from a royal lineage. We discussed the ZEESM project and Jose's involvement in the infrastructure rollout. He explained that the key to its success was that it had been working through the traditional governance structures in Oecusse. 'Even high-level political leaders are aware of this need,' he said:

They, too, understand that in order to develop Oecusse you need to know the correct way to enter into discussions, who to negotiate with and who to include. Otherwise nothing will happen.

Jose was clearly proud of his role in nation-building and keen to share with outsiders its success.

He explained a little of the history of Oecusse and how, from his perspective, this history underpinned current local power relations. Hundreds of years ago a foreigner from Malacca (with a Portuguese surname) arrived on its shores and married a local queen. 'Queens had great power then,' he maintained, 'because back then Oecusse society handed down power through the female line.' This royal marriage effectively brought a new powerful 'outsider in' to this society and changed the way of doing things from a matriarchal to patriarchal system. The new king also brought in more outsiders, which in turn much changed the region. These outsiders have all had key roles to play in the development of Oecusse. People from neighbouring islands of Rote and Savu were brought in to teach the locals how to distil palm wine. People from Alor, another nearby island, were brought across to teach people how to fish. People from other parts of West Timor were brought in as foot soldiers.

Jose described the three distinct classes of people in Oecusse today. The local people known as Meto mostly live in the mountains and still closely follow their customs and traditions, often including strict ancestral food prohibitions (e.g. depending on their clan, they may not eat chicken or fish or eels or prawns). The second kind of people are those known in Tetum as *lao rai sira* (travellers), the newcomers from elsewhere in Timor-Leste. These are townspeople. They are the bureaucrats, the teachers, the catechists and the traders (and many of the latter are Timorese-Chinese). Some of these people (including Jose himself) have married into the powerful royal lineages. Third, there is a class known as *kase*—foreigners, usually labourers, fishers and traders from elsewhere in the archipelago. 'It's been this way for a long time,' he said. 'Each class has their own culture and maintains their separate ways of life.' Each group, he added, is now adapting to ZEESM and benefiting in different ways. To get a better understanding of this, he offered to arrange for us to talk to one of his in-laws: the current king of Oecusse.

***

Photo 10: *Liurai* **Antonio da Costa outside his Pante Makasar house (with author).**

The house of Antonio da Costa, the *liurai* (king) of Oecusse is further down along the waterfront by the church of Santa Antonio, one of the first churches to be built on the island. The king's simple thatched house is built in a style known as *ume xinas* (Chinese house) and is very different from the style of conical thatched origin houses we had seen in the hills (*ume suba*). *Ume xinas* are built out of rock (or concrete) and *piku* (palm stem panelling) and have a long, narrow, thatched roof. The king told us that the house is a centre for ritual life in the region. Even today, all 18 of Oecusse's villages and associated clan lineages bring their post-harvest offerings here as tribute to the king.

This process was confirmed to us when we returned with our betel nut leaf, candles and rooster to visit Adelina's husband's family at the foot of the mountains. The rooster was sacrificed so they could 'open the door' to the ancestral or 'dark' realm and tell us some of the house's story. The family told us that if they (and the rest of their village) do not come together to take a portion of their rice and corn harvest to the king each year, the annual rains would not come. More than that, the springs would dry up, the crops would fail and the people would become ill. Along with their own household rituals, it was the king's divine connection to the entire nature spirit world that enabled them to properly communicate with and honour the localised spirits who inhabit their lands and waters. The king is, in effect, the living human embodiment of these custodian spirits. The family explained in detail their traditions and their past and present household struggles. Water was a critical issue for them, and in the dry season their own water source was more than an hour's walk away up hill. As we sat and chatted with the elders by the origin house, the younger men and women prepared the sacrificed chicken for lunch and a woman from the neighbouring house brought over a *tais* scarf she had just finished weaving. She had woven the words ZEESM carefully into its full length in large lettering. It wasn't my style, but I felt compelled to buy it from her.

Despite the ZEESM veneer weaving its ways into local society, it was clear that rural life here—as elsewhere in Timor—is still intimately connected to nature and its spirit realm. On the way back, we stopped at a nearby village to visit the workshop of Rosa and other women skilled in the tradition of handmade earthenware pots. The women in this area are renowned for their pottery skills, with each pot fashioned by hand, smoothed out by river stones, sun-dried, then baked in the coals and ashes of an open fire. They are then taken to be sold at the local market. The women explained the complicated process of acquiring the red clays needed for pot making. They needed to put together money annually to purchase a buffalo, which they would take to the site where the clays were sourced and sacrifice the animal to the nature spirits of the land. They also explained that, after collecting the clay and making the pots, each household must be particularly careful—careful that children not break the pots and that the money earned is spent on household necessities and not wasted. These responsibilities, they said, are a part of their agreement with the land spirits. Pots are provided to them as a household's sustenance, and pots enable them to put their children through school.

Before we left the potters, conversation inevitably turned to current politics. One of the women told us she hoped that Xanana Gusmao would win the next election. 'Only he understands the ways of old and old people's work,' she said. She scoffed at ZEESM and its leadership, saying that it had brought no benefit at all to her or her village. Manuel listened respectfully to the women throughout but was, of course, not pleased to hear this assessment. However, in the car journey on the way back, it was clear that he was somewhat torn in his support for ZEESM. 'The problem is,' he said, 'that the FRETILIN leadership do not know how to *kesi ema* [bind people], to bring people close and win their hearts.'

Photo 11: Rosa making earthenware pots.

As we drove back to town, we passed a pick-up vehicle full of youth campaigning for one of the minor parties. The militants in the back glared at Manuel, and he returned the glare. One of them yelled out indignantly: 'We are here to support the rice farmers!' Manuel's eyes flashed and widened: 'Go and eat rice forever, then!' he retorted. Farming was not a part of his vision for Oecusse's future.

Despite Manuel's ostensible modernism, on learning about my previous research in Baucau and other parts of the country, he had been very keen to introduce us to what he saw as important aspects of the cultural life of Oecusse. Before we left, he announced that he wanted to take us to meet someone else, someone who would help flesh out this deeper cultural story. So, at Manuel's instigation, before leaving Oecusse, we met with Paulo,[1] an elderly local historian of towering stature and another descendant of the royal lineage of the ancient kingdoms of Oecusse-Ambeno (a diminished version of which is represented by the current Oecusse-Ambeno special administrative region of Timor-Leste). Paulo was a descendant of the last king of Ambeno, Joao da Cruz, whose centre of power was not at the coast

---

1   This name is a pseudonym. Paulo did not want to offend his royal cousins.

but at a large *ume suba* in the mountains. This place is referred to today as 'parliament'. In 1912, Joao da Cruz had been driven out of Oecusse by the Portuguese and fled into Dutch territory where he had lived until his death in 1970. Prior to this, the kingdoms of Oecusse-Ambeno had extended from Soe to the east of Kupang to the Lois River west of Dili in Timor-Leste.

'After the arrival of Portuguese missionaries in Lifau in 1515,' said this descendant of Joao da Cruz, 'other kings became more powerful.' But he was careful to say a close relationship between all the ruling families has been maintained until this day. Nonetheless, he feared that ZEESM tended to presume that Oecusse is empty land. Indeed, he said, this is the very first mistake that they made. 'If they asked first,' he said, 'people would be happy to come to some accommodation with their development plans.' It was their presumption of the right to enter and reorder the world that would in the end, he thought, create obstacles for such initiatives. 'Especially in the mountains,' he told us, 'people still lay their faith in their spirit world.' They are not interested in development programs that try to change their practices and beliefs.

For my part, I left Oecusse a little shell-shocked. We had really only gone there to pass time while we waited for the bees to enter Lookeu. Yet, in less than a week, we had learnt so much about this tiny exclave, its history, its present and its possible futures. It was a rich, at times confronting and disorienting, visit. Although I knew we had only scratched the surface, I felt we had been privileged to learn so much in such a short space of time. Despite my own misgivings about ZEESM and its world-making plans, I left hopeful for Oecusse's future. One way or another its people would, I felt, work it out.

* * *

In May 2018, much to their surprise, FRETILIN were to lose both the popular vote in Oecusse and their hold on government nationally. To address widespread local concerns over the direction that governance of the territory had taken, the incoming government announced, in late 2018, a proposal to separate the ZEESM economic development program from the everyday administration of Oecusse. A shift of a new sort was underway.

3

Back Across the Border

The drive from Pante Makassar along the new coastal road heading east to the border with Indonesia was a little disconcerting. ZEESM billboards flanked the road for its full length, the main function of which was to advise local people that they were no longer allowed to build houses or dig along the coastal zone. The waterfront belonged to the ZEESM authority. People already living in the zone had been told that they would need to move. They were to be given other government land and new cement housing. Land outside the zone on the other side of the new road was already being bought up by private investors. There were plans for resort development. There was even talk of casinos and of international cockfighting rings and horseracing. The clientele was expected to come from elsewhere. 'People from Oecusse will be banned from casinos,' said Manuel. What exactly they would be doing, or where they would be going, was unclear.

We left Oecusse through Wini, the Indonesian town at this main border crossing. On both sides of the border, gleaming, shiny new buildings competed to outdo each other. The Indonesian side was especially impressive. ATMs, duty-free shopping and electronic scanning devices contrasted with the conditions at the tiny border post in the mountains.

Photo 12: Oecusse's main international border.

Upon exiting the immigration building, we were met again by our driver Patrice. As soon as we left the border area, we found ourselves in a small, dusty West Timorese seaside village. We turned inland and headed up a narrow road into a spectacular forested mountain range, broken up here and there by glistening manganese outcrops. On this side of the border the mountainous rural roads were again smooth and paved, if crumbling from washouts in a few critical places. We were travelling this mountainous route on the encouragement of Paulo, the descendant of the former king of Ambeno we had met back in Oecusse town. He had asked us to visit his ancestor's grave on our way back to Kefa.

When we had difficulty locating the gravesite, we stopped at a local administrative office for directions. The stocky official presiding over the office was very formally attired and peered at us a little suspiciously. When he found out that Quin was from Timor-Leste, he immediately relaxed. 'I am from Timor-Leste, too,' he beamed. 'I was pro-autonomy.' By this pronouncement, he meant he voted for integration with Indonesia as an autonomous province, not independence as a separate nation-state. Not quite sure about the implications of this statement, we nonetheless took the opportunity to explain that we were in search of the grave of the king of Ambeno.

Photo 13: Graves of the former king of Ambeno, Joao da Cruz, and his wife, Maria da Cruz.

The official, who had only just arrived in his car, stole a sideways glance at his driver. He made a quick decision and announced that he would drive us to the grave himself. We jumped in the car and he drove us at pace along a winding road for several kilometres. Thinking it was close by, we had left our car behind with Patrice and the kids waiting inside it. Finally, we stopped at a roadside kiosk, where he introduced us to an old man—also a descendant of the royal lineage of the king of Ambeno. We called Patrice and asked him to follow in our car. When they finally arrived, the kiosk owner quickly jumped in his aged jeep, and we followed him down another road full of twists and turns until we reached a small village nestled in the forest. We stopped at one of the village houses. The origin house next to it was much larger than the others we could see in the village. Behind the house we could make out a row of well-tended tombstones. They were the graves of the former king of Ambeno, his wife and assorted relatives.

We were welcomed warmly by the graves' caretaker and his wife. Many other women, men and children from nearby houses soon appeared to join us. They brought out chairs and a table on which they laid a brocaded cloth and offered us sweet coffee and coconut biscuits.

They were obviously delighted that we were visiting, that we were taking an interest in their history and, most significantly, that we had been sent by one of the king's descendants from Oecusse. The villages in this region, they told us, all consider themselves to be subjects of the king of Ambeno. At harvest time, a portion of the corn or rice harvested in each village would be brought to this origin house by the graves as tribute.

While we sipped coffee, we chatted about regional history and politics. The official who had brought us there suddenly chimed in with his own story. He told us that he was also from Oecusse and that he frequently returned there to fulfil his cultural duties at his family's origin house. But he said he couldn't go back there to live, not yet anyway. He declared loudly again with a broad smile and this time a fist punch in the air, that he was pro-autonomy. But this, it turned out, is not the reason why he can't go back.

Most of his family were supporters of FRETILIN in 1974, while at the same time another part of his family were supporters of Apodeti, a pro-Indonesian party. As a result, he had lived for some of his youth in West Timor. Then, when he had returned to live in Oecusse, he had been awarded a government scholarship to study agriculture in Bali. In Bali he became, like Quin, an active member of the East Timorese student resistance movement RENETIL. However, when he finally returned to Oecusse he was promoted to the head of the agriculture department. Landing such a good job, he told us, had persuaded him to a pro-autonomy position in 1999. After the vote, he, like most of Oecusse's population at that time, fled across the border and into these mountains. He had later worked with the United Nations High Commissioner for Refugees, assisting in the task of repatriating Oecusse's refugees, including his own mother and brother. He had wanted to return, but by then he had been given another good job in the Indonesian bureaucracy, so he had decided to stay on the west side of the border. His support for autonomy was pragmatic; it offered him a livelihood and security for his family. When he retired, he concluded, he would return to his homeland in Timor-Leste.

Throughout this extraordinary outpouring of the official's life story, the village people who had gathered around listened quietly and nodded in agreement. This man clearly had their respect as a local administrator and as a man who had to learned to work for both sides to survive. When Quin remarked that it was a shame that people along the border were physically divided, everyone agreed. 'Yes,' they said, 'we are all the same people. We share the same culture and history.'

Indeed, these peoples are so much alike and entwined in each other lives that there is a thriving illegal cross-border movement in the region. People without passports, or without the required documentation to apply for a passport, frequently *liu husi kotuk* (get through around the back) at the border posts. On the main Oecusse border, this process involves paying a small sum of money to an official to be escorted around the edges of the control area. 'Getting through around the back' is an option favoured by many East Timorese students who go to study in Indonesia. A formal border crossing requires that they pay and reapply for expensive three-monthly residency visas once in Indonesia. An informal crossing means they can, for another small sum of money, pay someone to organise them an Indonesian identity card. In these cases, their birthplace will be identified as somewhere just inside the Indonesian side of the border. Then they can stay in Indonesia as long as needed.

There is also a lively illegal cross-border trade in cheap fuel, timber, eggs and cigarettes into Timor-Leste. Meanwhile, cheap imported rice from Timor-Leste is smuggled into Indonesia. For a long time now, the government of Timor-Leste and foreign aid donors have been subsidising imported rice. People from West Timor frequently move across the border (legally or illegally) in search of labouring work. More worryingly, authorities are increasingly concerned that women and girls from Timor-Leste are being trafficked in the other direction into Indonesia.

* * *

After taking our leave from the house and the graves, we headed on to the Belu capital of Atambua to visit Balthasar's family and await the traditional honey harvest. In villages to the south-east of Atambua, the border with Fatumean in the Cova Lima municipality of Timor-Leste is clearly visible. Belu people frequently just walk cross the densely forested border to visit family and friends, to carry out ritual activities or to engage in trade both legitimate and contraband. Across this still remote section of the mainland border, a new 'international' highway, known as 'Jalan Jokowi', is being built under the mandate of Indonesia's President Joko Widodo. This planned 'super highway' will soon run the length of the remote mountainous border region. But, so far, it is unsealed and has little traffic aside from Indonesian military vehicles and locals crossing both ways to visit their families, with an 'administration' fee of around US$5 if they happen upon an Indonesian or Timorese soldier.

In this area of West Timor, people complain bitterly that their cattle are being stolen across the border by hustlers from Fatumean. Fatumean people are historically renowned for their cattle-handling skills. They are said to have magical knowledge and ingenuity that enables them to put a trance on even large herds of cattle. Once entranced, these cattle will simply follow their captors back across the border. While this is referred to as an age-old practice, the people of Belu are increasingly concerned that the illegal trade is enabled by a network of spies infiltrating authorities along the East Timorese side of the border.

Another of Balthasar's brothers, Hiro, is the family's cattle herder. Along with seasonal rice farming, Hiro spends much of his time out in the forested plains with the cattle. Having spent his entire life in these environments, he is impeccably knowledgeable about Lookeu and Fatumea (Fatumean) cultural traditions, about his family's lands and skilled in their agricultural traditions. Like Balthasar, he has never married and enjoys the time he is able to spend herding alone with his thoughts and observations of the area's often fickle tropical ecology. Yet it is increasingly difficult for him to find others willing to assist him with these daily laborious tasks. Unable to sleep at night due to continual worries about cattle theft and other misadventures, Hiro has considered simply selling the herd. Keen to stave off both the hustlers and the end of an era, younger brother Agus has more recently fitted out each member of the herd with a huge melodic cow bell.

Another cross-border problem that continues to affect the people of the Belu region is the 1999 influx of refugees from East Timor. During that period, thousands of people fled across the land border into West Timor. In most cases, people fled with groups of people from their own communities. Many settled down in government refugee camps along the border; others brokered their own arrangements with locals with whom they shared longstanding cultural and family links. While many have now returned to Timor-Leste, many more have stayed on. For some, the fear of reprisals is simply too great to risk returning to their home communities.

In the lowland village where many of Balthasar's family live, the population is around 1,600 people. Of that number, 600 are East Timorese refugees who fled there in 1999. They are known to locals as 'trans' (an abbreviation of transmigrants, although they were never technically part of the Suharto-era government resettlement program). The majority of refugees hailed from one village nestled high in the mountains of central Timor-Leste where the men were once foot soldiers for a feared Indonesian military unit.

The ancestral lands of the Lookeu kingdom spread across both sides of the border. Balthasar's youngest brother, Edmund, was, until recently, head of a village on the outskirts of Atambua. Married to a local school teacher from a neighbouring kingdom, Edmund had been elected in the late 2000s after the villagers decided to reinstate as their leader a son of the last king of Lookeu. Edmund was young and ambitious and, by 2018, he was immersed in the daily to and fro of Atambua region political life, hoping to be elected in 2019 to its district assembly. At the same time, he was deeply cognisant of his cultural responsibilities in living up to his father's legacy. I was coming to understand by this time how each of the Lookeu brothers played their own particular role in fulfilling this collective patrimonial legacy and promise: Balthasar was the cosmopolitan philosopher, Hiro the family's custodian of culture, Niko was the teacher and local intellectual, Agus was the adventurer, while Edmund was an aspiring regional politician. On the other side of the border, in the origin lands of Fatumea, the second eldest of the brothers, Deolindo, remained close by the ancestral Lookeu hearth.

Over dinner one night, Edmund explained to us how the dynamics of village relationships with the refugees from Timor-Leste has played out since 1999. In the beginning, the refugee camps created conflict with locals over land and resource use, specifically deforestation. In more recent years, however, there has been a reinvigoration of customary laws used in the formal governance of the village. He maintained that a major reason for this heightened enthusiasm for customary law was the need to deal with the dual problem of refugees and destructive resource use. Once it had become clear that the refugees were not returning to Timor-Leste anytime soon, customary leaders and others in the village power hierarchy realised that they needed to find a way to accommodate them that would work for both locals and the newcomers. Land conflict had been increasing and people were worried this would break out into communal violence. The leaders turned to customary law drawing on a process referred to in Tetum as *tara bandu* (to hang the prohibition).

Edmund had also arranged for a local *dato* (sub-village or clan head) to come to the house that night so that together they could explain to me their approach to *tara bandu*. I was familiar with the practice in Timor-Leste where, as a style of customary governance, it has undergone a revival in the post-independence period. It involves all parties coming together to carry out a communal sacrifice and to ritually and publicly agree to the terms of a land- and resource-sharing agreement. In this case, the pair explained, the newcomers had been given rights to farm in certain parts of the village, but not to own land. In addition, they were required to publicly recognise the rights of the current owners of the land. It was understood by both parties that, once this was done, the refugees would be welcomed into the community and allowed to draw from its common resources. To enforce the agreement, the parties would also participate in at least one community-wide ceremony each year. This annual ceremony would renew the commitments of intra-community respect, honour and sharing. Breaches of this agreement would result in fines and further ceremonies to be held at the cost of those at fault.

Edmund, whose relative youth also gave him a certain kind of cachet, explained that another matter that arose was the need to 'be tough with the younger generations', both those from existing communities and the newcomers. With his customary status beyond question, Edmund had begun a no-nonsense campaign to re-engage youth and enforce the return of the underemployed back to agricultural work. He maintained that this hard line had resulted in a renewed appreciation for farming. Meanwhile, the East Timorese refugees who now live permanently in the village made their livelihood from a mixture of market gardening, labouring to plant or harvest other people's rice, and labouring on road and other construction works.

As it was rice harvest season during our visit, we spent time in the fields belonging to Balthasar's brother, Hiro. This year, Hiro had, as usual, employed around 30 of the people who had arrived in the village from Timor-Leste in 1999. They were receiving US\$3.50 per day to harvest his rice. Without explaining the reasons why, most of them told us that they had not yet been able to visit their home village in the central mountains of Timor-Leste. Many had now built 'garden houses', often elaborate replicas of their origin houses (*uma lulik*) alongside their simple village homes.

As with many other East Timorese refugees now living in West Timor, their main origin house remained in their origin community where it is cared for by extended family members, many of whom the refugees had not seen for two decades. A lucky few of Hiro's harvesters had been able to host visits from family members from inside Timor-Leste. They said it was a lot easier to travel in from that direction. They didn't say as much but we guessed that this was because many of the refugee men in this village were ex-Indonesian army soldiers. Now living on Indonesian government pensions, they all said they still think of their homeland. To return might be risky and they would forfeit their military pensions. At least from their new village they could see Timor-Leste.

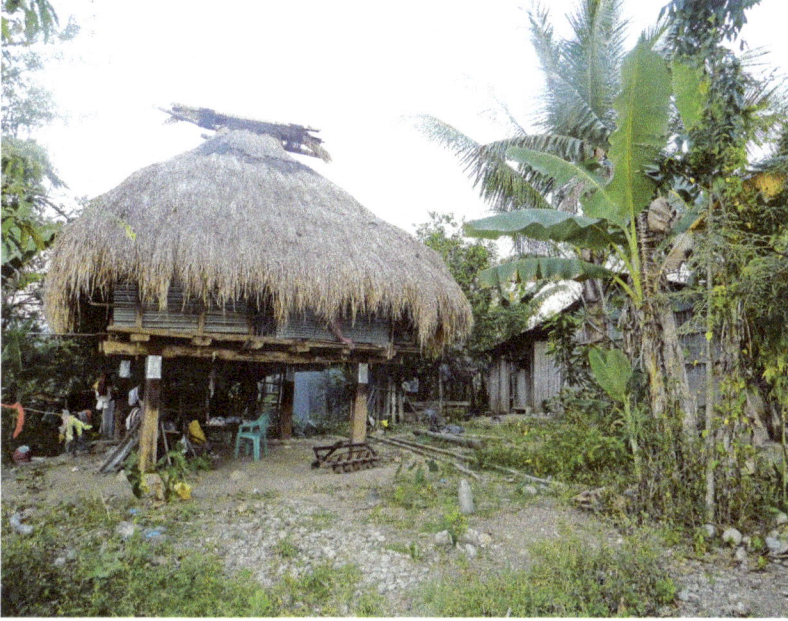

Photo 14: East Timorese 'garden house' in Atambua village.

The customary arrangements that allowed the refugees to stay in the village were not new. They are arrangements modified and adapted though a century or more of cross-border movement. In this village, the relationship between the local Tetum Terik–speaking community (who transfer land patrilocally through their father's line) and the migrant Bunak-speaking community (who transfer land matrilocally through their mother's line) is a case in point. A peaceful coexistence between various groups of these different language speakers in the village is enabled by the carving out of separate social spaces, a process referred to as *lulik malu* (a sacred agreement ensuring respect and harmony). In their daily interactions, people from either language group are prohibited through ancestral agreement from getting angry with each other, and from creating conflict or making onerous demands on the other group. If the cattle from one community eat the crops of the other, it is stipulated that there must be an amicable resolution to the conflict. Heated conflict would draw ancestral sanction—even illness or death—for both parties. At the same time, cross-marriage between the two groups is also accommodated, enabled by protocols that ensure the ongoing, respectful negotiation of difficult questions about whether a patrilocal or matrilocal inheritance and landowning system will be adopted—in many cases, these negotiations take place over years, if not generations.

Patrice lived in the Bunak-speaking community of Rai Ikun, whose people had fled in the 1900s from Taroman, a region of the Lookeu kingdom in Portuguese Timor. Rai Ikun people had a *lulik malu* relationship with the people of Lookeu. Patrice's family were not wealthy, but Patrice had inherited his parents' quiet determination and flexible approach to matters of custom and livelihood. They had come to the village from the Cova Lima region of Portuguese Timor in the mid-1970s. Even today, his family's origin house remains there. Patrice's mother was a Tetum Terik–speaker who married a Bunak-speaking man. In his own marriage, Patrice had chosen to marry a Bunak-speaking woman and had become a partial member of her origin house. Patrice and his wife frequently travelled back across the border to carry out ritual business at their respective origin houses.

Such movements back and forth for ritual activities are a common occurrence for both local Tetum Terik–speaking and Bunak-speaking populations in the village. While some have moved a new branch of their origin house into West Timor, others return to East Timor for all house-related business. Even those with a new origin house structure in the village will return to the main house in Timor-Leste for important ritual events.

I was struck by the apparent flexibility surrounding the governance arrangements and people movements along this area of the border. On the Indonesian side of the border, this flexibility is augmented by new administrative laws promulgated in 2016 by President Jokowi. The laws give Indonesian village heads significant powers and autonomy, especially around the regulation of land, water, resources, social relations and livelihoods. Yet, according to Edmund, the situation for the heads of villages in Timor-Leste is much more circumscribed. While customary processes are equally strong on both sides of the border, under Timor-Leste's new village governance system, village heads have, he believed, little to no real power under new national laws and processes and may be seen as puppets of the government. Even though their royal status makes his family the village's logical 'democratic' choice, none of his family on the other side of the border have shown any interest in becoming village heads.

4

Courting Bees in a Divided Land

'Bees are people', Agus had told us not long after we had arrived in Kupang back in April. This was the first fact I learnt about this animal (*Apis dorsata*) and its relationship to humans. In most years, April brings with it the end of the monsoon, yet, even though it was already mid-April when we had arrived in the province along the border area, heavy rain was still falling. Ironically, in a land often beset by drought and associated famine, the extended rainy season had delayed the blossoming of trees and brought its own kind of famine this year. '*Rai salaen*,' said Hiro, who was also in Kupang to meet us ('The land is hungry'). The ordinary Tetum and Tetum Terik word for hunger is *hamlaha*; however, here the high Tetum Terik term for hunger, *salaen*, is paired with *rai*, the term for land (and all that it is associated with). The utterance '*rai salaen*' conveys Hiro's highest respect for the subject under discussion.

Unlike Agus, Hiro had never been a *laku*. For one thing, he did not have the gregarious disposition that *laku* seem to require. The outlandish charisma of the *laku* was not the style of this regal and reserved more senior brother. Hiro had once been a foot soldier in the Indonesian army, during which time he had to fight against another brother, cousins and uncles who were fighting for FALINTIL. Now settled in the fertile valleys of his ancestral lands, just inside the Indonesian side of the border, he is a rice farmer and the extended family's cattle herder. From his fields and forest walks with the cattle each day, he can see clearly the mountains inside East Timor where his three older brothers were born, and where one of them still lives and another is buried.

This year, as the season transitioned from wet to dry, Hiro spent his days herding in the forest, watching carefully for the first signs of the bees' arrival. As he explained to me, he looks out first for the blossoming of a range of eucalyptus flowers, then waits to see if some bees appear in the land. These first bees, he explained, were the 'intel' agents sent ahead by the main colony to report on the state of the land and the prospects for the season's bounty. In a good season, by the time the bee swarms arrive the land will be filled with the scent of blossom.

The extended rains had interrupted the blossoming process and the *wani* (bees) had failed to enter either the land or the trees in their usual number. '*Rai salaen*,' Hiro said again. The land is hungry. He later expanded on another reason for this hunger. The people in this area of the border were now mainly farming rice and neglecting to plant the full variety of their more traditional agricultural crops like maize, beans, millet, sorghum, sweet potatoes, cassava and other root crops as well as pumpkin whose flowers are sought out by bees. I asked Hiro where the bees would be coming from. 'From somewhere else,' he said, 'from other forested lands across the island.'

Waiting for the bees to arrive had given us the chance to explore parts of West Timor and Oecusse. Reaching Atambua (Tetum Terik: Atanbua) and the international border in early May, we were hopeful that we had been able to coincide our visit with the seasonal honey harvest. Balthasar had now joined us on the border. We were in the mountainous village of Lookeu, within the kingdom of Lookeu, where Balthasar's paternal grandfather and his people had fled in the early twentieth century after being forced out of Portuguese Timor by the colonial state. Earlier, during a war in 1896, the colonisers had destroyed the Lookeu Palace and centre of government inside Portuguese Timor.

In the house built by Balthasar's parents, we were introduced to the village head, Kanis, a young man educated in Kupang and a nephew of Balthasar. We chatted over coffee and biscuits and betel nut as people started to arrive to greet the oldest son of the last king of Lookeu. (Balthasar, who lives in Melbourne, had not been home for six years.) The house was right next to the Uma Metan Lookeu, the elaborately thatched main origin house and present-day palace of the Lookeu royal family. From where we were sitting, we could just see a ridge that was obscuring what is now the international border between Indonesia and Timor-Leste (see Map 2). Mikail Asuk, one of Lookeu's ritual leaders, explained to me later that night: 'We are from Fatumea [inside Timor-Leste]. Two countries, but one ancestor.'

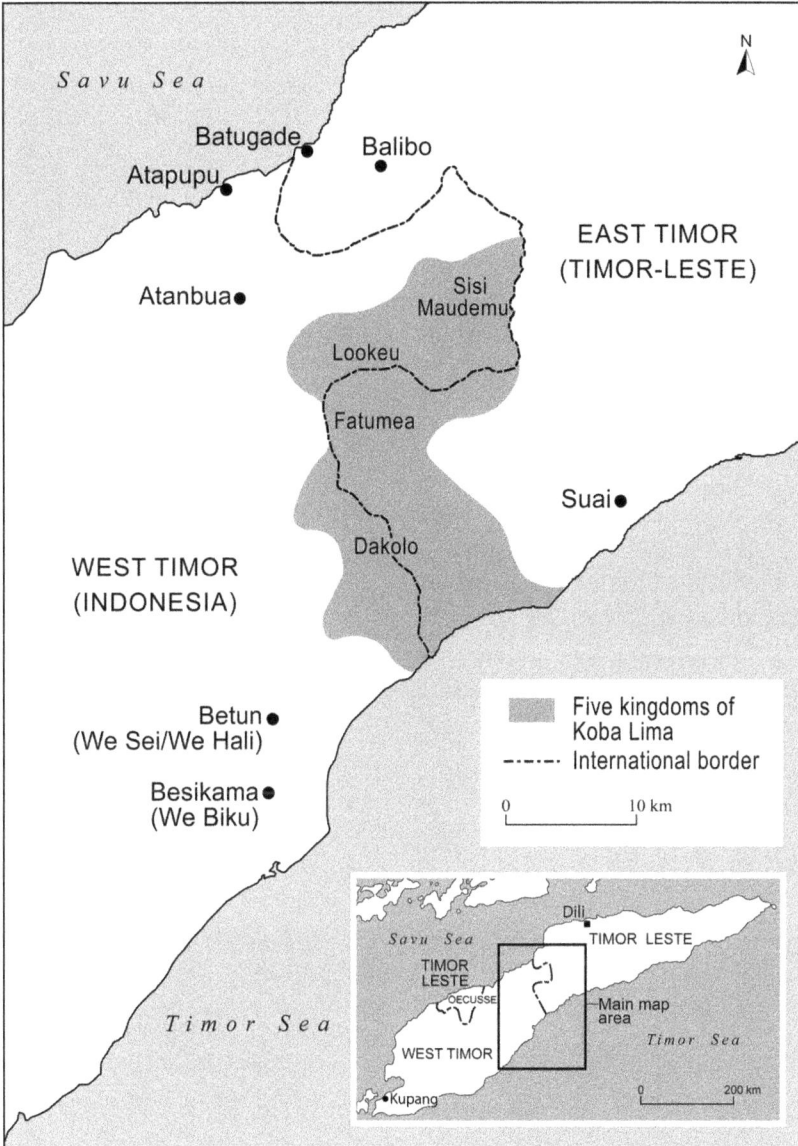

Map 2: Location of Lookeu, one of the five kingdoms of Koba Lima.

Source: Chandra Jayasuriya.

Earlier, Balthasar had recalled the tragic circumstances of his father's movement back and forth across the colonial border:

> In Dutch Timor my father was imprisoned by the Dutch, when he was still single, for his recalcitrant spirit. He later went across the border to our land and people of the Lookeu Kingdom in Portuguese Timor. He married my mother and settled in his own ancestors' land and among his own people of Lookeu. Opposing the Portuguese, he was arrested, tortured and jailed. He refused to be treated as a common man and demanded to be recognised and treated as a king in his own land and among his own people both in Dutch Timor and Portuguese Timor. He was also against the abuse of young women by the head of the Portuguese army and government in Fatumean. He refused to allow his two beautiful sisters to be used.

Not least because of this personal history, this was an emotional visit to Lookeu, a chance for those present to share stories of the past and rekindle relationships. It was also a chance to retell narratives of suffering on the border, especially during the tumultuous years following the Indonesian occupation of East Timor. Then, thousands more people fled across the border where they became caught between opposing Indonesian and FALINTIL resistance forces. Two of Balthasar's schoolmates from Indonesian Timor, suspected by the Indonesian army of being FALINTIL spies, were beheaded in front of the Uma Metan Lookeu. The beheadings were carried out using a sword gifted to Balthasar's father by an Australian solider during World War II. After the beheadings, the villagers were ordered to bury them. These stories were retold, I sensed, for at least two audiences. One was me, a foreigner; another was my husband Quin, a fellow Timorese from the far east of the island. They wanted him to know that it wasn't only those inside East Timor that suffered.

Kanis told us that there were now about 1,000 people living in the village. All of the refugees who came from East Timor in 1999 had since returned. Most of these refugees had come from Fatumean, just across the border. These people were family and the pathways are always open for them to return.

All of Balthasar's family and the other villagers in Lookeu were clearly thrilled and honoured to have him back in the village. We were taken inside the Uma Metan Lookeu and shown the house's male and female pillars where the lineage's ritual offerings are made. In 2006, when the house was reconstructed, the huge trees needed to fashion these two pillars had been cut down in the land of Lookeu inside Timor-Leste. From there they had been carried by hand across the border by teams of extended family members from both sides of the border. The logs were all the while adorned in male and female ceremonial attire and, by the laws of the house, they were not allowed to touch the ground until they reached the site of the origin house's construction.

After our talks and a walk around the village, including an emotional visit with village elders to the ruins of the former palace built by Balthasar's paternal grandfather during the Dutch occupation, we returned to the house and began our conversations about the upcoming honey harvest. I was told this would be a small harvest, to occur over a matter of hours, not the usual grand event where one tree might have up to a hundred or more houses and require up to seven *laku* and most of the night to harvest. I was introduced to one of Agus's childhood friends, Domi, who owned the wild almond tree (*Irvingia malayana*) that was to be harvested. He told me that his grandfather had planted the tree some 50 years earlier. Domi, like Agus, had been a *laku* in the past and he proceeded to regale us with humorous stories of his and Agus's youthful tree climbing and honey misadventures. (Most of the laughs came at Agus's expense.)

Later, Domi took Balthasar and me aside and quietly told us that 'the bees have names: Buik Lorok and Dahu Lorok'. Female names. (Buik is also the name of Balthasar's older sister. Dahu is the name Domi's younger sister and the name of a female cousin of Balthasar. Lorok refers to the sun, as well as to divinity or 'the enlightened one'.) Domi repeated what I had heard on my arrival in Kupang: 'the bees are people'. Their queens are Buik Lorok and Dahu Lorok and it is they—and people's relationship with them—that we were to celebrate at the honey harvest. He explained that the *laku*'s job is to sing to the queen bees, and that through this serenade they would recognise their connections.

The songs were ritual love songs. Domi explained that they are sung to touch the hearts of these female bees and entreat them to return to their home year after year. He added that if these songs are not sung and the ceremony is not properly carried out, Buik Lorok and Dahu Lorok will not return. As proof, he told us that one of the other main honey trees in Lookeu had its 40 hives improperly harvested during the last honey season and, consequently, no bees had returned to it this year. Harvesting properly means harvesting communally, with song, dance, offerings, ceremony and prayer, leaving in place some of the hive for its immediate rehabilitation if the bees so choose. At the end of the season, when the bees have departed, the trees would be 'cleaned' by their owners. While some of the wax is left, the old hives are removed, and the branches are smoothed off so that the queen bees and their 'houses' will return—and, it is hoped, invite other newcomers to make their 'houses' in the tree.

I had been wondering why the ritual was called *hola wani* (literally meaning 'to take the bees'). In Tetum, while you can say *hola* meaning to buy, take or exchange something in a shop, you can also talk in the vernacular about 'taking' a woman or a man. This means to secure a wife or a husband through the marital exchange of specific cultural goods and communal ceremony. I wondered what it meant for people to *hola wani* (take bees)? Was there some kind of marriage-like exchange happening here between people and bees? After all, I had been told that bees are people. Now I knew the songs sung were highly poetic love songs, intended primarily for the female bees. And the *laku* were demonstrably the most charismatic, brave and agile of men.

Back in the village, as I pondered these musings, an unseasonable heavy rain began to fall. I knew that such unexpected 'natural' events are usually linked to ancestral intervention; they happen for a reason. I enquired into the significance of this event. 'It is bringing us *matak malirin* [a greening coolness].' The ancestors were rejoicing that the oldest son of the last king had returned.

Prior to the honey harvest, Balthasar had participated in a ceremony to welcome him back to the house. This ceremony also involved as many of his siblings and their children as were able to attend. Collective participation would ensure the prosperity and good health of the entire lineage. On the night of the ceremony, we began by making offerings at the family graveyard close to a ridge that obscured the international border. There, family members lit candles, prayed and sang at the graves of their ancestors. One grave belonged to Balthasar's paternal great-grandfather, Moruk Kehi, the king of Lookeu who fought against the Portuguese in 1895. But only his head was buried there; his body was buried at the place of his death in Portuguese Timor. Also in this grave was Moruk Kehi's wife, Sawak Funan, the queen of Kowa (in Balibo). Other graves held Balthasar's grandfather, who had founded the present village of Lookeu, and Balthasar's parents.

Photo 15: The palace of Uma Metan Lookeu.

When we finally entered the palace of Uma Metan Lookeu, the first offerings made at the male and female pillars were areca nut and betel leaf. The men sat on the male side of the house and the women on the female side. Baskets with betel offerings were placed in other sections of the house, including on the border between the male and female division and the outside altar. These offerings honoured the connection between Balthasar's lineage and the kingdom's mountains, fields and springs. After an hour or so, a group of young men carried a medium-sized black pig up the ladder into the house. It was slaughtered over the entrance door and its various body parts became part of an elaborate ritual and feast. Later, the presiding ritual leader, Mikail Asuk, mixed droplets of the pig's blood into a paste with betel chew. Beginning with Balthasar as guest of honour and ending with us (the visitors), each was called to enter the male part of the house where Mikail Asuk blew his breath onto our foreheads and pressed onto our sternum and forehead small portions of the potent paste. This was to ensure that Balthasar and all those in his company would exit the house with *matak malarin*—a greening coolness and flourishing life energy.

At that time, it was well past midnight and Madalena and Zeca were fast asleep in the car, but then someone mentioned that the children's heads had clipped the thatch as they had entered the house via an opening in its low thatched roof, the edges of which extend almost to the ground. Such contact is *lulik* (forbidden) and elders were worried for their spiritual safety. So, before parting company for the evening, Quin and I accompanied one of Balthasar's brothers to wake the sleeping pair. We roused them just enough that they could properly receive their blessing of greening coolness. Any danger following from their inadvertent breach of protocol had been ameliorated.

Photo 16: Ritual inside Uma Metan Lookeu.

After a few hours sleep we were out in the forest with Hiro, Domi and the other *laku*, cutting bamboo for the evening's harvest. First, we cut the wild bamboo that, with its thorny side branches, makes a perfect ladder to ascend tall trees. Next, we cut and segmented another kind of bamboo that would be used to cook the harvest offerings of rice, beans, meat and bee larvae. Then we removed bark panelling from two blossoming eucalyptus trees so as to fashion the trays required to knead and strain the honey. Finally, we cleared the area around the forest stone altar where the food and honey preparation would take place.

As our party rested by the altar, I decided to ask Hiro more about the nature of the relationship between people and bees. As I was formulating the question, as if from nowhere, the senior ritual leader, Mikhail Asuk, emerged imposingly from the forest. Balthasar took the opportunity to question him on my behalf, and Mikhail smiled wryly, saying: 'They descend from one people, but of these things we cannot speak; we must be silent.' I was a little crestfallen. 'Don't worry,' Balthasar reassured me. 'Hiro knows these things and we can ask him later.'

In the meantime, Mikhail explained to us his role in the evening's harvest ritual:

> The bees and the honey harvests go back to the time of our ancestors, but I cannot climb like a *laku*. When the honey harvest season comes, I travel everywhere around here. When the time comes for the bees to arrive in our land, the owners of the bee trees will ask me to come and call the bees. I will also be asked during each harvest to attend so that then I can communicate with them and ask them to come back next year. This skill is gifted to certain of us in Lookeu.

The bees come each year to Lookeu from named places: from the Turiscai mountains of the Mambai-speaking people in East Timor, and from the lands and mountains of the Dawan-speaking people around central north-west and central-south of West Timor. 'The bees from Turiscai are small,' Mikhail said, 'just like the people who also live in that part of the island.' Before he rose to take his leave, he remarked that the bees we would meet during the night are also warriors. 'Our ancestors prayed to them and used them in war,' he said.

Photo 17: A *laku* begins his climb.

As night began to fall, people began to emerge through the darkness into the light of the fire by the forest altar. The three *laku* who would climb this evening had already tied the bamboo ladder to the tree. They had attached it using forest vines to lash it to the top of a small tree from where it was laid crossways and strapped to the upper trunk of the much taller honey tree. The set-up looked precarious. When the first *laku* leapt across to try it out, he ensured his success by singing out to the bees at the top of his lungs—something that both gave him courage and let all in the vicinity know that the harvest was about to begin. Back at the forest altar, the bark honeycomb tray and a palm-fibre filter had been positioned so that the honey would flow along it and down through a bamboo half-pipe into the plastic honey bucket below. Smooth-flowing honey would indicate the night's successful harvest and signal the life blessings to flow forth through the community from the bees.

Photo 18: The black stone basket offering.

Dozens of villagers were now gathered in the forest. They began to prepare the 11 offering baskets and assorted ritual adornments that would be presented to the bees prior to the harvest. Among the offerings was the *fatuk metan* (black stone) basket specifically for the queen bees, Buik Lorok and Dahu Lorok. One of the senior men wrapped this basket carefully in a black cloth and adorned it with five corn-sheath cigarettes. The pungent smell of these hand-rolled cigarettes would entice the bees down from the tree during the evening's harvest.

Once the black stone basket had been prepared, we carried it in procession to the base of the tree where it was further adorned with *morten* (a red coral bead necklace) and *belak* (golden breast plate). Another two of these ritual objects were hung from a notch on the trunk of the tree.

One of the *laku* assumed his role as lead singer of the offering party. As he stood at the base of the tree, he began a resounding sacred love song to the bees. Soon he was joined in chorus by many others who held hands around the base of the tree. The linking of hands reflected both their bonds to each other and with the bees. The singers circled the tree three times, exhorting:

> Ooooh … ooooh … ooooh … *fatuk metan* [black stone] … eeeeh … the wild almond tree where you hang yourselves, where you come to dwell. You came together here as a group to make your home … We bid you a farewell … do come next year. Tonight, we are here with you, our generous and respectful lovers, Dahu

> Lorok and Buik Lorok. You are giving us your sweetness and the strength of your bodies. We are here to thank you and to bid goodbye to you while hoping and pleading for you to return next year. To return here to your home so we shall be together again for another night. So that we can taste your sweetness and the strength of your beings … Do kindly share your experience in this home to others and bring them along next year, too.

As the singing and movement concluded, the *laku* held aloft the black stone basket and rotated it in the air in the three directions from where the bees had come, and to where they would return.

The deep emotion of the serenade resonated through the forest and our bodies. The excitement was building. Next, a small black pig that had been tethered to a stake nearby was carried across to the base of the tree for offering. Domi, the honey tree's owner, rubbed the animal with betel leaf to give it the blessing of life, before another man respectfully and skilfully slit the pig's throat and drained the blood into a bucket below. Domi moved in the shadows between the pig and tree base, collecting drops of the blood with betel leaf, which he rubbed around the trunk of the tree and over the various other ritual offerings. When it was done, the offering baskets and the dead pig were carried back to the forest altar.

Now the *laku* were ready to climb. Lulled into an unhurried sense of time during the day's slow preparations, we realised that we had quite suddenly reached the climax. We scurried back to the forest altar where we had left our bags, and the children and I put on protective clothing that someone had presciently suggested we purchase the day before in the district capital of Atambua. Everybody else, including Quin, remained in their shorts, sarongs and t-shirts. 'Don't worry,' I was told, 'bee bites are like medicine. They make you stronger.' In the ensuing hours, I would come to be so thankful for my recently purchased blue plastic raincoat, matching pants and camouflage ninja mask.

When the *laku* started to ascend the trees and began to vocalise, all was fine at first. We stood and watched, awestruck but calm, from the forest floor. 'Ooooh,' sang out the *laku*:

> We have prepared the rope to climb … we have tied the bamboo ladder … we are on our way up … you are all hanging up there waiting for us … ooooh … our beloved, enlightened Dahu and Buik Lorok.

Photo 19: Honey harvest fire blooms.

The *laku*'s song was, however, soon punctuated by hissing sounds as their firesticks, now alight, brushed against the first of the hives hanging down from the branches above. The sparks from this contact flashed out spectacularly into the darkness, forming wide blooms of red before beginning their descent to the forest floor. This, I had been told, was cue for the bees to do the same: to follow the light of the sparks, to descend and lie quietly on the forest floor so that their remaining sweetness could be harvested.

Because we were also filming the event, we were using torchlight to enable the recording. As a result, the bees were now also flying en masse towards this alternative source of light—and anyone standing near it. What felt and sounded like rain on my plastic jacket was a hail of bees. They came in waves, in unison with the work of the firesticks above. By this point, I was filming mostly with my eyes tightly shut, as everyone was yelling out for us to do. I would sense when each subsequent wave was arriving by the intense bodily reverberations and smell that would precede them. This olfactory cue would then be quickly augmented by the sharp pain of searing hot needles piercing my gloved, camera-holding hands. Mikhail's words rang through my head: 'These bees were also used by our ancestors as warriors.' This truly felt like a war zone.

But when the camera was not in use and the torches were switched off, peace returned to the forest floor. We would be serenaded again by the red blooms and the ritual love songs of the *laku*. The peace was punctuated by the occasional calls from old men on the ground, entreating the *laku* to secure a date for next year with their beloved bees. Alternately, keen for the harvest to be filmed, these same senior men would periodically call out to admonish the other ground-dwellers to stop their banter. 'Be quiet! We are SHOOTING,' they would yell. All during their exchanges, a pulley system of buckets was being used to convey the honeycomb from the high branches to the ground, where a small team of men were waiting to collect it and, amid the swarming bees, carry it off to the forest altar.

Most people, including our two children, had now retreated to the forest altar about a hundred or so metres from the tree. Some sat chatting by the fire; others were helping to cut up the pig and cook the various cuts of meat with rice and beans in specially fashioned bamboo cylinders. One old man had the job of kneading and straining the collected honeycomb, while others stood by to watch how it flowed. These tasks were in full swing by the time we returned to the altar with the *laku* and the last of the comb. The people seated by the fire were happy; their reading of the pig's liver was positive and so all was in order. Just as importantly, the kneaded honey was flowing well along the bark, through the fibre strainers, down the bamboo half-pipe and into the bucket. These were auspicious signs for the agricultural year ahead.

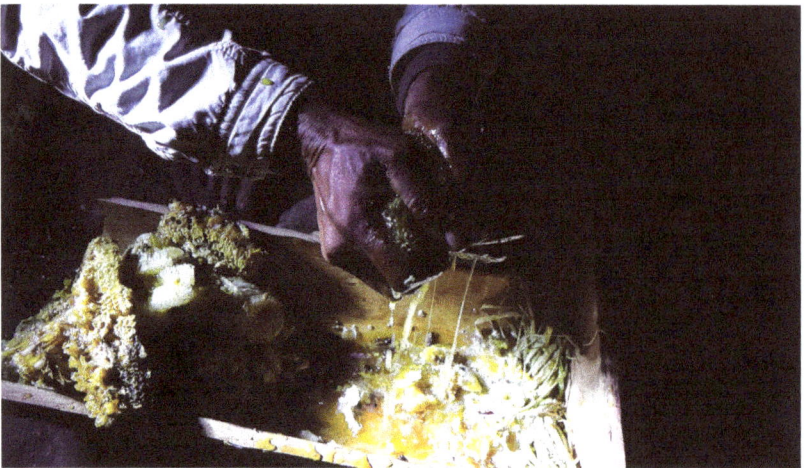

Photo 20: Straining the honey.

After the offerings had been prepared and laid out in each of the 11 offering baskets, we carried them back to the base of the tree. All of the baskets except the black stone basket with its betel nut and cigarettes had been filled with rice, beans, meat and slivers of the harvested honeycomb and bee larvae. The bees were still hovering around the base of the tree, and they swarmed us again. I had been sweating profusely inside the plastic raincoat and hadn't realised we would be heading back into the war zone, and so I had prematurely taken off my protective clothing. 'Don't worry,' the others told me again. They explained that if we held the right attitude and composure the bees wouldn't sting (much) and those that did would give us a dose of medicine, making us stronger. This time it worked; I didn't get a single sting.

After we had honoured the bees and their spirit custodians by placing the cooked offerings at the base of the tree, we picked up the baskets and returned to the forest altar. There we all sat and ate together by the firelight before each receiving a piece of the life-blessed betel nut to take home. We collected up the remaining honey, beeswax and larvae-filled combs and carried them back through the night to Domi's house where the spoils of the harvest would be shared out among all involved.

In the past, this honey would be shared among families, sometimes traded with others. We had been told that there is now a thriving commercial market for wild honey. If the honey and wax harvest is plentiful, the *laku* and the tree custodian, who receive the largest shares, will often sell some to Chinese-Indonesian traders in Atambua. In the modern supermarket near our Atambua hotel there was even a display of assorted honey products near the checkout, with one brand labelled 'Timor wild honey'. A 200 mL bottle sold for around US$2.

The day after the ceremony, when we were back driving around Atambua, I had the chance to ask Edmund (Balthasar's youngest brother) about the white bag of honeycomb he had carried back from the tree late in the harvest. At that time, he had called out to us excitedly and pointed to the contents of the bag. 'This is the *lulik* [potent] one,' he had said, bringing it over so that I could film inside. 'Look at the body of that comb,' he marvelled, before pointing out the *morten* and *belak* in the same bag.

These were the same two ritual objects that had been carried up into the tree by Bruno, one of the *laku*. Edmund explained, as if I already should have known, that this was an act of *fo folin* (giving value), a process used to describe the ritual goods given in marriage exchange by a male house to the house of a man's bride. Here in the honey harvest, the goods had also been carried up into the tree as an offering to the female houses of the bees (and later brought down again, with the very best of the honeycomb). *Hola wani*, I then realised, meant 'to court bees'. What we had just participated in was an age-old Timorese process of courtship, only this time it was of bees, and the ritual took place in a divided land.

The painful pairing of courtship and division in the practice of *hola wani* reveals the consequences of history. Although these types of honey harvest ceremonies were once carried out right across island Timor, it is only in the most remote and mountainous areas that the practices continue. Wars and displacement since the imposed colonial division in 1859, deforestation and changes in land use and crop composition are rapidly changing the island landscape and its attractiveness and carrying capacity for bees. Ironically, the suffering and displacement experienced by the Lookeu community along both sides of a remote and once dangerous mountain border has also kept others out and allowed the survival of relatively intact forests that are so essential for their continued relations with wild honey bees. Through the ritual of *hola wani*, the people on the border of island Timor demonstrate both their determination to maintain the bees' movement across the region and to preserve their shared identity.[1]

1   The 30-minute film documenting this harvest is called *Wild Honey: Caring for Bees in a Divided Land*. It is distributed by Ronin Films.

5

The Politics of *Lulik*

My visa for another land-border crossing into Timor-Leste was to expire two days after the honey harvest. It was time to go. But we had not anticipated the challenge of securing a rental car to take us across the border and on into Dili. The Indonesian rental company were highly reticent. The Timorese national election was scheduled to be held in three days time. On the day we were to travel, the ruling FRETILIN party would be holding their final mass rally at a lake on the edge of Dili that was on our route into the capital. Meanwhile, people in Atambua had been speculating about the likelihood of election-related violence. The rental company was spooked. As well as being worried about their car, they couldn't find a driver willing to take us to Dili. Just as we were about to give up, they secured the services of Paulus, a driver from Kefa who travelled into Timor-Leste regularly. As we piled our belongings into the brand-new vehicle, Paulus was ordered to maintain close phone contact with Atambua along the way.

We eventually left West Timor and began the drive of three hours or so along a relatively new road from the main border crossing to Dili. It was my first time travelling through this north-western part of the country. Even though the wet season had recently ended, the relatively sparse vegetation already felt dry and crackly and the lowland hills were parched. Apart from the many sago palms and the variety of wandering livestock, we might have been in the north Australian savannah. For lunch, we decided to make a detour from the coastal road into the mountains up to Balibo, the town infamous for the murders of five Australian journalists by invading Indonesian forces in 1975. This detour, we figured, would also buy us some time in our attempt to avoid the roadblocks and the political rally in Dili.

Photo 21: Flag house with painted Australian flag in Balibo.

We stopped first at the famous flag house in Balibo where the young journalists had filmed each other painting an Australian flag on the front wall. A vain hope, as it turned out, that their foreignness might protect the group from the impending invasion. Because of the resolute fight by their families and supporters to bring the Australian and Indonesian governments to account for their deaths, Balibo is a name many Australians recognise. It is often one of the only things they know about Timor-Leste. In a personal twist, we had only recently found out that a cousin of one of the Balibo Five lives over the back fence from us in Melbourne. Even though I knew the history of the Balibo Five well, it was unexpectedly moving to visit the actual site of their deaths. Visiting the house where they were murdered was poignant but, for me, it was somehow even more shocking to discover the view from the refurbished ruins of the nearby Balibo Fort. Looking down the mountainside from the old stone walls of the fort, it was evident how close we were to the Indonesian land and sea border with Timor-Leste, the place where the Indonesian gunships had anchored and helped launch the 1975 land attack. Despite the intervening 40 years, our proximity to the site of this initial invasion made it more real and still terrifying. The deaths of these five journalists was not the only reminder of Australia's connection to the Indonesian invasion. A recent book by Kim McGrath has argued that Australia's pecuniary interest in the Timor Sea oil and gas reserves dates as far back as the 1960s. Australia's support for the ensuing Indonesian occupation can be read in this light.

Photo 22: View from Balibo Fort.

As I mused over this history looking out across the walls of the refurbished Balibo Fort, Quin had met some old friends who had stopped by the fort cafe for coffee. When I went over, they were deep in discussion about the impending election. They were political party organisers on the campaign trail and said they were not discounting the possibility of violence. Quin and I returned to the table where the kids were seated, quietly ate our lunch and we continued on.

As we neared the capital, it was apparent that some of the hillier sections of the new coastal road were already cracked and subsiding. 'Clearly,' our driver said, matter-of-factly, 'they didn't do the proper ceremonies to ask the spirits of these places for permission to build the roads. So, this is what they get. Crumbling roads.' I wondered if the roads on the West Timor side of the border were so good because they had carried out the required ceremonies and secured the requisite ancestral permissions? But before I could ask, he launched into a tirade about the Timorese political election. 'It's just like a football game!' he exclaimed. 'The only question is, do you go for Barcelona or Real Madrid? Just like in football. East Timorese go mad for their chosen party. Actual policies don't matter.'

It was near dusk as we approached the lake at Tasi Tolu, the site of the final FRETILIN party electoral campaign rally. Despite our best attempts to avoid such timing, we arrived just as the rally finished and campaigners were spilling out en masse onto the main road. Our path was logjammed. We feared it would take us hours to travel the last few kilometres into Dili. Madalena and Zeca, who had been asleep, woke up as the vehicle came to a near standstill. It was a rude awakening. All we could see outside the car was guns. The roadside was filled with military soldiers, military police and regular police. All were in full combat gear and all seemed to be clutching semiautomatic weapons. We told the kids to relax; this was normal election security in Timor-Leste (which was not exactly untrue). It wasn't the first time that day, though, that I had worried about the situation we were going into with our kids.

Our Indonesian driver was petrified. He decided that our best option was to stick close to an open police vehicle containing two rows of heavily armed military police. I was not sure this was the best approach, given that it would put us right in the firing line. But proximity to the armed forces seemed to calm our driver and we continued towards Dili. In the end, all was fine. The traffic started to move much more quickly than we had anticipated and, from there, it was not long until we arrived at our hotel, where, despite our invitation to take refreshments, the driver quickly bolted for the safety of his company's compound on the other side of the city.

In contrast to the Indonesians' trepidation (and much of the international commentary), the people we met in Dili, including Quin's family, reassured us that we needn't have worried. The pact between the security forces had held throughout the recent campaign. It was only if the security forces started turning on each other, as had happened back in 2006, that we would need to worry. Indeed, as we had driven through some of the coastal villages earlier in the day, the atmosphere had been almost festive. At each house lucky enough to have a television, crowds of people were gathered inside and out, intently craning to watch the final televised campaign spectacle. When we stopped for some freshly roasted fish in one village near the Loes River, we found the roadside eateries with televisions were also filled with crowds of locals. This village was obviously not a FRETILIN stronghold. Entire families had gathered around to watch, and all were vocal in their commentary, ridicule and criticisms of Prime Minister Mari Alkatiri's final campaign speech. Yet the criticism was matched by the certain intensity with which people were listening. As he concluded his speech, Alkatiri's final words—'Keep the peace, respect democracy and respect the electoral process'—drew grudging respect and perhaps a collective sigh of relief from the television viewers. Despite the lively atmosphere and the ridicule, these were the calming words everyone had been waiting to hear.

Just one day earlier, many of the same villages would most likely have been deserted. The rival party had held their final campaign rally at Tasi Tolu and it too was televised and streamed on the internet. After we arrived in Dili the next night, Quin and I watched the recording of the coverage on hotel wi-fi. Viewing the footage of the rally, it was clear to us that the coalition known as the Reform Alliance Party (AMP) were at this stage campaigning on something of a *lulik* (ancestral power) ticket. The AMP alliance featured three heavy-hitting leaders: resistance hero, former president and prime minister Xanana Gusmao; former president and FALINTIL commander Taur Matan Ruak; and rural youth and mystic martial arts leader from the central mountains, Naimori. Through their speeches it became apparent that the three had aligned themselves (and their political campaign) with the three sacred mountains of Timor-Leste. In this consubstantiation, Xanana's power was linked to the country's tallest mountain Rame Lau, Taur with Matebian, the 'mountain of the dead' in the east, and Naimori with the third tallest mountain, Cabalaki, which was the early twentieth-century stronghold of Dom Boa Ventura, Timor's first 'nationalist' hero.

Taur spoke first. In an impassioned speech, he told the frenzied crowd that the problem in the previous elections a year earlier was that the parties who comprised the new AMP alliance had campaigned on separate tickets. None of the parties now comprising AMP had won, because their separateness and disunity had displeased the ancestors. Now he affirmed that the parties had come together, assuring the elated crowd that with ancestral backing the AMP would surely form government.

Next Naimori spoke. His words were *falun* (poetically wrapped) in the style of the richly coded botanical metaphors contained in the ritual poems of Timor's traditional orators and origin houses. In these cultural metaphors, every pathway can be traced back to a powerful source and for a path to be successful the source must be acknowledged and embraced. Naimori spoke of trunks and branches and new sprouting tips, of the roots of life (the ancestors) and possibilities of flourishing life for those people who voted for AMP. His speech invoked AMPs connections to the ancestral powers of the natural world, a world that he, too, claimed would undoubtedly support the AMP to victory.

During the rally, Xanana Gusmao was singled out by both Taur and Naimori for the greatest praise. They both referred to him as Timor's greatest-ever leader. Xanana himself did not make a speech at the rally. Instead, he chose to take on a role akin to that of court jester, humouring and exciting the crowd with his larger-than-life body language and antics. All the while, Xanana said very little. He didn't need to speak; his mystique and power preceded him.

Some commentators said that the enigma of Xanana had clearly been reborn in this election campaign. His CNRT party had lost power unexpectedly in the previous year's elections on what might be considered a modernising ticket of progress and mega-projects. The president had given the FRETILIN party (who had won the most seats) the opportunity to form minority government. Devastated by the shock loss, Xanana had left the country for many months. He justified this absence as necessary for him to focus on renegotiating the Timor Sea Maritime Boundary Treaty that would finally resolve the decades-old oil and gas dispute with Australia. At a distance, Xanana began to regroup politically. Back in Dili, the new minority FRETILIN government was faltering. They could not pass their budget and the funds needed to deliver even basic services were running out during a political stalemate over the budget negotiations. It was then that Xanana pounced. He summoned his former political rivals, Taur Matan Ruak and Naimori, to meet with him in Singapore. From there, the three leaders held a joint press conference, announcing the birth of a new coalition that would hold FRETILIN to account. For a while, Xanana was nicknamed the 'tele-commander'. It seemed that the writing was on the wall for the Alkatiri government. An election was called in 2018, around the same time that, against the odds, a new maritime boundary with the Australian government was announced. Xanana returned to Dili, victorious and ready to campaign again to take power.

***

When things go wrong in the lives of Timorese people, they generally return to their roots. Problems are addressed by opening up channels of communication with their ancestral *lulik*, a realm ordinarily forbidden and taboo. In difficult times, people concentrate on summoning their resources to carry out the necessary rituals and to implore their ancestors and potent nature spirits to redress their suffering. Was this what Xanana was doing when he regrouped with the AMP alliance? A reframing of his modernist vision through a *lulik* alliance signalled a return to his cultural roots that assisted in regaining his waning charisma. This power comes not only from inside Timor-Leste, but also from outside: people speak of Xanana's predilection for visiting *lulik* sites and finding audiences with mystic leaders across the Asian region. While these encounters are understood to run much deeper than political opportunism, they are also common populist strategies in Indonesian political campaigns.

The *lulik* alliance worked the crowd into a frenzy at that final campaign rally. I was told emotions had also run high at earlier rallies in places like Oecusse. People spoke about this election as being akin to the popular referendum in 1999. They likened it to a second national referendum on the future of the country. Despite the high stakes, it was never clear to me, and many others, how different the FRETILIN and AMP policies actually were. What was most obvious was the leadership styles of the two rivals and their difference in abilities to reach out to people and draw them in. In this regard, Xanana was peerless. Mari Alkatiri was widely known and respected, by supporters and political opponents alike, as an astute manager. However, even his supporters recognised his lack of charisma and inability to connect with the people. In Oecusse, his technocratic governance style ultimately proved both unpopular and detrimental to the FRETILIN agenda. I was told of a woman who pleaded to Xanana through her tears at the AMP rally in Oecusse: 'Why did you give us to Mari?' Ironically, this woman and the others wailing and hugging him at the rally knew only too well that the ZEESM project they were bemoaning was of Xanana's creation and the speculation was that it was proffered as a kind of peacemaking gift to Mari after FRETILIN lost power in the post-2006 political crisis. Yet banishing Mari Alkatiri to Oecusse had backfired. He had used ZEESM as a platform to return to the national stage and, on the back of his own modernist agenda, he had staged a political recovery. The promise of modernism could, however, only take each of these leaders so far. Now, in Oecusse at least, the people wanted Xanana back.

Many Timorese who hailed from the east of the country had a more cynical view of the self-styled *lulik* alliance promulgated by the AMP. The east of the country remains a FRETILIN stronghold. This was the heartland of the armed Timorese resistance during the occupation, and people continually refer to the fact that their ancestors died for the revolutionary FRETILIN flag and no other. Our conversations with easterners in the days prior to the election revealed a deep ambivalence about the AMP's politics of *lulik*. One veteran of the resistance told me that *lulik* was undoubtedly the reality of life in Timor-Leste. FALINTIL fighters always knew that they must both honour and harness the power of *lulik* to secure victory. Those in the east had laid their lives on the line for both their ancestral lands and for the FRETILIN flag and they had won the war only because their ancestors were backing them every step of the way. This man said that people from the west of the country (the locus of AMP's largest support base)—people who 'did not actually fight for independence'—were only now coming to understand this reality.

Others from the east whispered that it was not a positive *lulik* behind Xanana's latest push for power. This time, they believed, his power had its source in something much more sinister. Rumour was rife that a malign supernatural force (*biru*) had taken over his body and this powerful force was feeding Xanana's return to power. As with any such form of spiritual exchange, it was understood that he must feed it in return.

According to some, the source of this *biru* was spirits from outside of Timor-Leste—malevolent spirits, sometimes specified to be female, that had captured Xanana's soul and made him a prisoner to their demands. Ideas about such malevolent forces pervade Timorese political life and their need for sacrifices is evinced, in such accounts, by recent Timorese political history. Former president José Ramos Horta was nearly offered up when he averted death from a rebel attack following the 2006 political crisis. Horta's would-be assassin, renegade military commander Major Alfredo Renaldo, was instead shot dead during the attack (some attributed his death to a bewitching by a glamorous girlfriend). Another renegade ex-resistance leader, Mauk Moruk, openly challenged Xanana's authority and was killed in 2015 by a military operation. Even the untimely heart attack and death of Fernando La Sama, former student resistance leader and leading national political figure in Xanana's government, could be read as a sacrifice to insatiable *biru* appetites pervading the political scene. Given these supernatural forces at work, it was understood that Xanana's power would only grow stronger. His longevity already attested to this. Even his fiercest critics believed there was nothing he could not do. According to these FRETILIN supporters, Mari now needed to exercise extreme caution; his managerial brilliance was simply not equal to the *biru* enveloping Xanana. These claims were not so much personal as a pragmatic recognition of the darker power of *lulik* and the supernatural. If you honour it and pay your respects, it will support you. If you go against it, look out.

Xanana's resistance history has been well documented in a biography by Sara Niner, but lesser known fragments of this story and its post-independence pathways continue to be evoked or reworked in conversations across the country. While in West Timor, I had watched an online video in which Xanana explained to a new generation of viewers his connections to the ancestral world. The story revolved around the origins of his bestowed first name, Kay Rala. (Xanana is his nom de guerre.) In the video, he is filmed in conversation with a young female reporter explaining an incident in the early days of the resistance. On patrol outside of the town of Manatuto area, he and his ragtag band of fighters had stumbled on a small swidden garden where there lived a very old man. At the time, Xanana and his men had only 12 guns and 16 spears between them. The old man came out of his house to speak with them and immediately recognised Xanana. It turned out that during the Japanese occupation, this old man had hidden Xanana's town-dwelling parents and provided them safe haven in his home. As a result, the old man, who was also a mystic, knew the details of Xanana's family lineage and history.

At one point during their encounter, the old man had asked Xanana if he really wanted to win the war. 'Yes, of course,' replied Xanana. 'Well,' said the old man, 'if so, you must change your name. Jose Alessandro is a Portuguese name, a Catholic name—if you carry that with you, you will only die early.' He proceeded to tell Xanana that he could keep his family name of Gusmao, but that he must chose a different first name. He gave him a choice of two indigenous names from the family's ancestral lineage: Kay Rala or Kay Olok. Only these names had the capacity to *fanu bei-ala sira* (to wake up the ancestors) and give Xanana the strength, endurance and power he needed to win the war. It was from that moment that Kay Rala Xanana Gusmao came into being.

Wherever you travel in Timor-Leste, conversational anecdotes will link Xanana with the *lulik* or ancestral powers of particular places. The greatest claim a healer can make to the efficacy of their practice is that they once healed Xanana, or one of his family members or associates. In the far east, I was once told a story offering another explanation as to the source of Xanana's formidable power during the resistance. In despair at the deaths and suffering of so many of those around him, Xanana had decided to travel across to the far eastern island of Jaco, in the company of a local mystic. One night, as evening fell and the tide receded from the island shores, Xanana walked with the tide back towards the mainland. He walked as close as he could to the deep-sea channel that lay between Jaco and the mainland. In the language of Fataluku, Jaco is known as Tortina, meaning 'to be cut off', a reference to the act of a maritime-based ancestral being who severed the island from the mainland. This division created a channel, a place where it is said that the island's south male and north female seas most potently mix. It was there, by the channel of one of Timor's most auspicious sites, that Xanana began to incant a ritual prayer to the ancestors, whereupon an ancestral grandparent crocodile rose out of the deep water, opened its mouth and gifted something (perhaps a crocodile tooth?) to Xanana. Whatever its material form, the immense power of this object turned around the prospects of the resistance movement. Xanana, I was told, carries this object with him to this day.

Photo 23: The channel between Jaco (Tortina) and mainland Timor-Leste.

Yet my Fataluku friend who related this story and many other East Timorese insist that Xanana lost the respect that ought to accrue to someone with so much power. He had done too many deals, let down too many people and brought into his inner circle too many former pro-autonomy people—people he now controlled, but who weakened his power. The pro-independence leaders left on the outer were people he could not so easily control. An AMP campaign rally in the capital of the far eastern district of Lautem was poorly attended. Some youth even protested Xanana's presence, a response that two decades earlier would have been unthinkable.

According to those who give credence to ideas about malevolent spirits linked to Xanana's resurgence in power, the church has also knowingly distanced itself from Xanana. Yet warfare between the supernatural forces of the 'dark world' is not something that the church—a product of the light—can openly countenance. Similarly, the theory goes that the FRETILIN leadership cannot talk publicly about *biru* and the supernatural. They, too, are people of the light—modernists—and their talk is about the need to find out facts. During the campaign and immediately after the 2018 election, the FRETILIN leadership was preoccupied with revealing the truth behind Xanana's reported electoral manipulations on the campaign trail. But everyday Timorese critics of Xanana know that the FRETILIN leadership won't be able to find this data; the evidence simply cannot be produced. Xanana's power to mobilise support from the supernatural world draws on the services of beings so tiny they are not even visible to the human eye. They, these critics believe, are the ones who get inside things like voting booths and business contracts and manipulate outcomes. They have the ability to change things like election results, monetary sums and the names of payees. They leave no evidence because they are invisible. And it is because of this invisible support that Xanana will always win. The suggestion is that Xanana has, in effect, succumbed to their will. According to this scenario, the FRETILIN leadership are merely unsuspecting do-gooders in a battle between good and evil.

Later, when Xanana and his AMP alliance triumphed over FRETILIN, those who believed in such malevolent spirit theories also expressed their concern for Mari. Despite being part of his vanguard of support, they say that he would be better off accepting the result. 'Other leaders—like Mari—can't do anything. Mari can't win. It has now been proven beyond doubt. He is simply not powerful enough.'

I discern some deep politics in these accusations, framed as they are by particular worldviews. Yet these views are also slippery and complicated, arising from no single source or agenda. They are indicative of the deep spiritual politics bound up in expressions of *lulik*. The politics revolve around claims to national political legitimacy and an even deeper politics, centuries old, that can be traced back to the power struggles between Catholicism and indigenous religions. In the symbolic and material battles between the so-called forces of darkness and the forces of light, darkness represents indigeneity and the fickleness of the ancestral world, while the light is modernity and the salvation offered by Christ—and, increasingly, economic mega-projects like those in Oecusse.

Xanana's political rhetoric of oil and gas riches and mega-project development in the country holds out the promise of the light. So, too, does FRETILIN's technocratic agenda. Yet, Xanana's hold over the East Timorese people is of a different order. His is a power deeply enmeshed in Timorese ways of understanding the world and in their everyday ancestral practices. People in Timor believe in the powers of *lulik* and of their ancestors, as they believe in the agency of malevolent spirits (some of whom might be angered ancestors) to control others and to wreak havoc. The power of *lulik* is extremely potent and always influential, invoking fear, awe and at least begrudging respect. The spirit world has power to do good as well as ill, and it can turn on people and make them captive to its whims. Xanana—not the man but rather the public figurehead—represents these processes and more to different people, in different ways, at different times. He, more than any other person, embodies both quintessential Timorese power figures and the paradoxes of darkness and light, tradition and modernity.

6

Small Island Sojourns

In the uneasy quiet of the election's aftermath, we decided to travel to Atauro, a tiny island about an hour's speedboat ride from Dili. The formal election result was not expected for another a week or so, and there remained a chance of trouble in the interim. Some people predicted that, if there were to be disturbances, they would be in Baucau—and we were en route to Baucau. Even though the people we knew in Baucau were not concerned about trouble, we decided to err on the side of caution and spend a few days on an island detour.

As it transpired, vote counting on Atauro had already taken place. The island had fallen by a narrow margin to AMP. Our speedboat arrived on the island at the same time as a large police boat that had come to collect the votes. We heard that militant FRETILIN youth in Dili were so outraged by the result they had vowed to wait at the wharf for returning university students from both Atauro and Oecusse (which also fell to AMP) and to teach these traitors a lesson in loyalty and gratitude. Given that Atauro was the second 'development hub' of the ZEESM project, and the island usually voted FRETILIN, the incumbents had expected to win.

As soon as we alighted from our boat, we heard from villagers of ZEESM's plans (under Mari Alkatiri) to clear the waterfront establishments in the village of Beloi. We were told that, in anticipation of development, a number of national leaders had purchased land in the hills just behind Beloi, even though until recently most hadn't set foot in Atauro for years. The villagers said that Mari Alkatiri's younger brother's company oversaw most of the roadworks and construction on the island, and his involvement seemed to be borne out by the dusty construction company sign we later saw outside a house on the main road.

Photo 24: Women sewing inside Boneca de Atauro.

We alighted from the speedboat near Barry's Place, a lush and homely eco-resort right on the beach and an obvious drawcard for *malae* (foreigners). Our pre-booked accommodation was in what turned out to be the very sleepy main town of Atauro, Vila Maumeta. We made our way there by a three-wheel taxi that sped through the parched coastal landscape on the best dirt road on the island. (There weren't many roads on Atauro and all were unpaved.) Our guesthouse, Manu Kokorek (crowing rooster), took its name from the island's main mountain towering above. Opposite the guesthouse is the Boneca de Atauro (Atauro Dolls), a women's co-operative. We had already seen a film about these soft cloth dolls made by Atauro women, so we were familiar with the business. Our kids owned several of their dolls back in Australia. The next day the co-op was in full swing and humming with around 60 women working slowly, but industriously, on their foot-controlled Singer sewing machines. The dolls come in various colours, all dressed in brightly coloured offcuts of *tais*, with details handsewn by the small groups of women seated on the beachside veranda. Fabrics were strewn around the co-op in various piles, with the inside cupboards full of merchandise awaiting shipment to Dili hotel and airport gift shops. The women worked intently, occasionally breaking out into conversation or hilarity. Most, we learned, walked two hours each way down the mountainside and then back up just to get to and from work. Yet, despite the hardship of this extended commute on foot, and the cooking, housework and childcare that awaited their return home each day, we could feel their shared pride in this creative small business.

Manu Kokorek and Boneca de Atauro, and a range of other small businesses mainly run by women, were established after independence with the help of two Italian priests, both of whom had previously worked for decades in Brazil. The women we met told us with pride that the priests had a very hands-off approach—they would show people how to do things once and then leave it to them. In this manner, they had helped to establish a range of co-operatives focused on traditional medicine, sewing, knitting, cooking and jewellery. In the guesthouse where we stayed one of these priests had taught the staff how to make homemade pasta and gnocchi. Italian food was now the specialty of the guesthouse's restaurant. Later in the year, we watched a screening on Timorese television of a Brazilian-made film, *Priests of Atauro*, that documented the activities and passion of these priests on the island.

***

Despite countless trips to Dili, we were visiting Atauro for the first time. This was an unexpected diversion from our planned onward journey to Baucau and I had no research plans other than checking out the island as a possible alternative site visit for one of my annual university field classes. I had always been interested in finding out more about a story connected to one of the island's springs that I had heard frequently during my research into springs, people and culture in Baucau. However, this was an old, possibly ancient, story, and I did not really expect it to be familiar to people living now on Atauro. People in the eastern coastal village of Wani Uma had told me the story of the 'migration' of one of their springs called Wai Krang. This spring site was now dry in Wani Uma due to an incident in the distant past between feuding brothers. An intra-family conflict had resulted in the older brother excluding the younger ones from a rice harvest ceremony. The ceremony had begun while the younger siblings were pulling their fishing boats ashore. When they looked up at the ridge where their sacred house complex was situated and saw the smoke of the fire billowing up, the younger brothers, knowing that the ceremony had begun without them, decided to leave the region. They packed three dugout boats with goats, chickens and people before visiting the spring of Wai Krang to ritually collect water in a bamboo length. Then they sailed their cargo-laden boats west until they reached Atauro. There they settled and 'replanted' the waters of Wai Krang to produce a much-needed spring on the largely dry island. I stood on the coral reef shore near our guesthouse and tried to imagine the scene of their arrival. Right next to where I stood, an older man sat staring out to sea on the beach in front of his house, its wide-open doors revealing an altar filled with carefully arranged nautilus and other shells. We exchanged a brief greeting and I would have liked to have opened up a conversation with him, but Quin was back at the guesthouse and I sensed the man wasn't too keen to speak any further with a lone female *malae* wandering the beach with her kids.

Later, I asked Leocadia, the hardworking host of our guesthouse, if she knew this man and the Wai Krang water story. She explained that the man lived there alone and was something of a recluse, rumoured to be captive to the spirit of a deceased lover. To my surprise, Leocadia also knew of the water story. She explained that it belonged to the family of one of the women who worked in the co-operative. We had already planned an afternoon walk with Leocadia to take in the view at the Catholic grotto atop a nearby hill. Leocadia suggested we call in on the family connected to the story on our walk.

My work in Timor often takes such unexpected turns. To arrive in a place with a premeditated research plan is always frustrating and generally not fruitful. In contrast, moving through and within places with an open, meandering approach allows for unexpected encounters and happenings. It is through these events that the specific interests of my research can organically unfold, actively infused as well by the interests and concerns of the people and places I encounter. Of course, this approach provides no certainty, takes time and requires much patience. Timorese people do not usually expect foreigners to be interested in or to be able to understand their deeper cultural concerns. Frequently, it may feel as if not much is happening at all. Then, just as frequently, a rapid-fire range of experiences or conversations will provide dizzying insights and tantalising, but always elusive, details into a range of matters. The process is akin to being swept up in a whirly-whirly, a kind of informational and relational spiral that sweeps in and oversaturates my senses at the same time as providing insights that I know I must try to hold on to. I long too, in these moments, for the calm after the storm and much-needed time and space to reflect.

Photo 25: Quin and Jose.

After the sun's intense heat began to wane, we set off. Along the way, I enquired about a sign on the front of a building along the main road indicating that it was a traditional medicine co-operative. Leocadia said we would stop in at a place selling Atauro medicine further down the road. She took us to the house and introduced us to Maria, a slight, middle-aged woman who had been one of the founders of the traditional medicine co-op. For a number of years I had been researching traditional healing practices and ethnomedicinal knowledge in Baucau, and so I was very interested to hear more about Maria's practice and experience. On the other hand, I was keen to keep going because I didn't want to miss out on meeting the family with the connections to the spring of Wai Krang. I mentioned this need to keep moving to Quin and, as we rose to take our leave, Leocadia gestured over to Maria's husband. Almost as if it was an aside, she said: 'And this man—well, he is one of your fellow compatriots from Baucau.' Jose was descended from one of the brothers who settled by Wai Krang. He even looked like a younger version of Nai Usu, the angular, sharp-eyed ritual specialist we knew well in Wani Uma.

We explained to Jose our interest in the story of Wai Krang. He confirmed for us that his ancestors did indeed come from Wani Uma (house of the bees) in Baucau. Three brothers came in three boats. He explained that, along with the spring water, they brought with them a knowledge of ceramics, a craft that was until then unknown to the people on Atauro. They also brought with them bees, who made their hives inside that of the brothers' origin house. Impressed by their gifts and new technology, the Atauro owners of this stretch of land gifted the brothers an area of their own. This parcel of land, which stretched in a narrow strip from their landing site on the coast up into the mountains, is still owned by the 'Baucau' clan today. Jose told us of two springs on his land—one is now dry, but the original one the ancestors 'planted' still flows. (The origin house his ancestors constructed by the spring no longer stands. Instead, his clan now have a smaller house closer to the coast where they carry out annual rituals.)

According to Jose, the ancestral connection between Atauro and Wani Uma is widely known on the island. Some time ago, a woman from Atauro married a man from a village in Baucau near Wani Uma and lived there for several years. But contact between families from the two places is *lulik malu* (forbidden): they are banned from close relations; they cannot drink or eat from each other's houses nor can they be involved in each other's rituals. As it turned out, this injunction extended to us. At one point, Jose mentioned that he was a renowned palm wine maker, but when Quin asked if he could try some, Maria interjected to say that there was none left. Later, we found out they were too scared to give it to us.

A similar reaction occurred when we asked if we could go and visit the spring. Maria intervened again in the local language and warned her husband to be careful. Leocadia later explained what Maria had said. 'It's too risky. These people are also from Baucau; they could be related.' Jose diplomatically told us he would take us another time. In fact, he said, if we wanted to know more about the spring he would need to gather together the representatives of the other brothers' houses to meet with us as well. Only when all three of them were present could they properly talk about such things.

As we walked up the steep and rocky incline behind the village to the Grotto of Our Lady, Leocadia pointed out a tiny thatched structure, like a miniature origin house, perched on the hillside. 'That's the place,' she said, referring to the house where Jose's clan carries out annual rituals. We would later discover that the spring itself was only a couple of hundred metres from the main path up to the grotto, and that Leocadia knew its location, but she had decided during the walk that she was fearful to take us there.

When we returned from the grotto down the hill, Jose was waiting outside his house. He said that he had decided he would accompany us through the village and back towards the coast to show us the site of his ancestor's original boat landing. I presumed he would lead us right down to the beach, but instead we stopped by a large tract of empty scrub on the roadside. As we were by then about 200 metres inland, we were puzzled to learn that we were at the boat-landing site.

Photo 26: Atauro coastline.

Much later I discussed the boat-landing site with one of my Australian colleagues, a physical geographer. Russell Drysdale is a specialist in geomorphology, climate and sea level change. From my description of the site's geography as about a metre above sea level, Russell estimates that the site might have been at sea level around 1,000 years ago. This is our first clue into the period of the brothers' arrival on Atauro, and the relative age of the story I had first heard in Baucau almost 10 years earlier.

Until the Indonesian invasion, the original anchor had been in place at this landing site, but Jose told us that the Indonesians forced the locals to move it and, as a result, it had broken into pieces. But, miraculously, the anchor had reformed as a whole when the pieces were placed inside the tiny origin house up the hill, where it remains. This origin house must be refurbished each dry season. Jose explained a ritual involving the sacrifice of a goat and the calling of the name of Cape Bondura (a powerful ancestral site near Wani Uma in Baucau) to ensure the arrival of the annual rains. I was stunned to hear this. Cape Bondura is also known across the wider Baucau region as the site of the region's most powerful rainmaking ceremony. At Cape Bondura, however, the ceremony has not been done for decades.

Photo 27: Cape Bondura coastline, Baucau.

As we stood by the desolate first landing site, Jose lamented the fact that the area is too *lulik* (potent) to be occupied. The site itself is situated in a residential street, but nobody has dared build anything permanent there. Once a neighbour tried to set up a carpentry business on the site, yet an accident occurred during construction and the man nearly died. Since then, it has remained empty. Jose was trying to find someone (a ritual specialist) to help him move the *lulik* potency of the site further inland, just as they had relocated the anchor at an earlier time. As a descendant of the ancestors who arrived at the site, Jose figured that he should be able to build a house there. 'But right now,' he said, 'I am still looking for a pathway. It is not an easy thing to do.'

***

Maria told us that the priests had helped set up the co-op. They had brought with them knowledge and seeds of certain medicinal plants from Brazil and had shared these with the group, encouraging them to plant the medicinal plants on the island. Maria said she liked the way that the 'priests gave their knowledge with their hearts; the way they opened their hearts to us'. In contrast, she said: 'Our ancestors, who also had powerful knowledge about plants and medicines, kept it hidden. Anything we found out we were told to keep secret.' The priests instructed her not to *subar* (hide) her medicine anymore—which was why, as she proudly indicated, her medicine was there on display in a lockable cabinet on her front veranda. 'I put it there for all to see,' she said. 'Should people wish to buy some, they can do so.'

When we returned to our guesthouse that evening, we met up again with Maria. This time she had come to visit us, bringing some medicine that Quin had ordered from her and that she had spent several hours making. She showed us carefully how the migraine tonic made from the boiled bark of a tree should be drunk. Standing up, she poured some of the medicine in a cup and showed us how to take small sips, holding the chin at just the right angle while imbibing the medicine. We both noticed that Maria was buzzing with energy. She proceeded to thank us profusely for coming by her house and talking with her, for being interested in her work and for buying her medicine. Maria told us that for the first time in a long time, she had 'come out from under the table'. Even better, she firmly felt as though she had 'found a place at the table'. She went on to say with obvious emotion that, because of our encounter, 'I felt again, for the first time in a very long time, that I was a person; that I was a woman again and I could be proud'.

Photo 28: Maria and her medicine cabinet.

As she talked, we slowly came to understand what she meant. Maria had some time ago ceased working alongside the traditional medicine-making co-operative. She explained that she is a very hard worker who makes and sells a wide range of medicines and who has frequently travelled to Dili to treat people. 'What's more, I am brave,' she said. 'I have cured many people.' For this reason, some others in the community were jealous and began to scorn her, blaming her for deaths including in her own family. Since then, she had stopped taking an active role in the co-operative and had withdrawn into her own world.

Across Timor, traditional medicine is a practice associated with the 'dark' spirit world or, more pejoratively, in some Christian circles, with the work of the devil. This was a reason why practitioners such as Maria, who clearly had more medicinal knowledge than she had learnt from the priests, was attracted to working in the co-op. To be able to tell others that 'the priests taught me' gave practitioners the ability to circumvent the discrimination and prejudices extended to traditional healers. Atauro is known across Timor as a site of powerful medicinal knowledge and practice, and a place with many *matan dook* (those who see far)—healers and sorcerers associated with the 'dark' arts of the ancestral and nature spirit realm.

Although Maria was quick to stress to us that she is not a *matan dook*, her experience of community scorn suggested that such accusations are never far from the surface. The church plays an ambivalent role in this domain: it is often the source of the prejudice; at other times it offers practitioners, particularly females, refuge and respite from the very same accusations.

***

A few months later, back in Baucau, I had the chance to recount our meeting with Jose and Maria to the village head of Wani Uma and to one of the village's *matan dook*. Under the baking sun, seated in the village head's front yard with a view across the sea, they both listened with great interest to the tale of our encounter. Then the healer got out his notebook (an old pocket diary) and began flicking through it until he found a page with some names he had carefully written down. He read them out. The village head nodded in agreement, confirming the names of the three brothers who left by boat. These names have been preserved in ritual and, more recently, in the notebook to this day. The village head recounted the story to me again. 'The brothers were from the house of Watu Naru,' he said referring to his own house, which is associated closely with Cape Bondura:

> They took the water inside the bamboo, as well as a branch of the *sabao* tree. When they planted the water on the island, they also planted the branch of the tree. The tree grew and so the people on Atauro knew that these men had come with clean hearts and intentions.

He corroborated the story Jose had told of the woman from Atauro who had married someone from the next-door village to Wani Uma. One day, said the village head, as she was collecting firewood, she unwittingly entered the area of the Wani Uma origin house complex on the ridge. 'She immediately started having problems with her vision,' he said, 'a sure sign that she had come too close.' He reiterated that the lineages are still forbidden to each other. Talk of repairing relations had been entertained in the past, but in the end it was decided that it was just too complicated.

I was left wondering about the link between the name of the village Wani Uma (house of the bees) and the story I had now heard of the brothers arriving in Atauro with bees. I had been told by another Baucau ritual specialist, Major Ko'o Raku, how, in the beginning, a seven-headed bee had arrived in the region from across the sea, bringing with it culture and the institution of marriage exchange. Yet the people of Wani Uma had always refused my questions about the significance of bees and it was only on Atauro that I learnt that bees were intimately connected to the origin stories of Wani Uma houses.

7

Underground Flows

After returning from Atauro to Dili, we hired a car and set off for Baucau along the windy, narrow coastal road. In one section, the road hugs the steep cliffs so tightly that any small driving error risks the vehicle plunging several hundred metres into the tranquil blue waters below. The Portuguese-era road was under reconstruction in places and the dust-filled, 100 km journey took us five hours.

Baucau is my husband's hometown. The country's second 'city', it has a population of around 20,000 people and comprises a Portuguese-era old town and an Indonesian-era new town and bureaucratic centre. The picturesque old town is built into the edge of a limestone escarpment and the new town sits above that. Towering over the coast at about 600 metres above sea level, the old town consists of four villages interspersed with terraced rice fields, groves of breadfruit and coconut trees and the verdant foliage of the ficus and areca palms surrounding lush tropical springs. These springs are fed by diffuse underground flows of water percolating through the landscape from the drier plateau hinterland above.

Many parts of the old town contain caves, craggy limestone outcrops and springs. Quin's family home is right in the centre of the old town, very close to the town's main water supply, the spring of Wai Lia. I first heard stories of the nearby Wai Lia spring from my father-in-law. As I dug deeper, more stories emerged, and they have captivated me ever since. My father-in-law (or Apa, as I called him) told me that when the Indonesian soldiers retreated from the town in 1999, the Wai Lia spring had suddenly sprung back to life. It had been near dry for many years, and yet, as the Indonesians withdrew, it once more gushed forth, feeding the town's depleted water supply and channelling irrigation waters to the terraced rice fields below. Apa explained that these waters were rejoicing, joining with the people in celebrating this unlikely Timorese victory. The ancestral forces of this spring had, he told me, long given spiritual assistance and power to local people in their resistance activities. I was intrigued. I wanted to find out more. And so started a very long journey to do so. Water, as I learned, is a constant shapeshifter and connector. As is evident in the story of the spring's resurgence following the retreat of the Indonesian military, it is understood to have agency, sentience and personality. Springs move across the landscape with people—sometimes even taking the form of people.

The further I delved into these various oral histories of the spring, the more I realised that the stories I was being told of Wai Lia changed across time and space. Drawing them together revealed sometimes bewildering insights into human connections to this limestone environment and its watery flows. Yet, despite their conflicting accounts of history and associations, at their core they were about the determination of Baucau people to honour and respond to their dynamic relations with this place and its human and non-human inhabitants.

***

Each year I take a group of university-level geography students on a study tour of Timor-Leste. When we visit Baucau, I organise for the various *bee na'in* (water custodians) of Wai Lia to gather together with us and recount their version of the spring's story and discuss its implications for ongoing water management in the town. The students are told that Wai Lia spring has its source in a cave called Wai Lia Bere far up on the Baucau plateau. This is the same story that I heard when I first began this research in 2006.

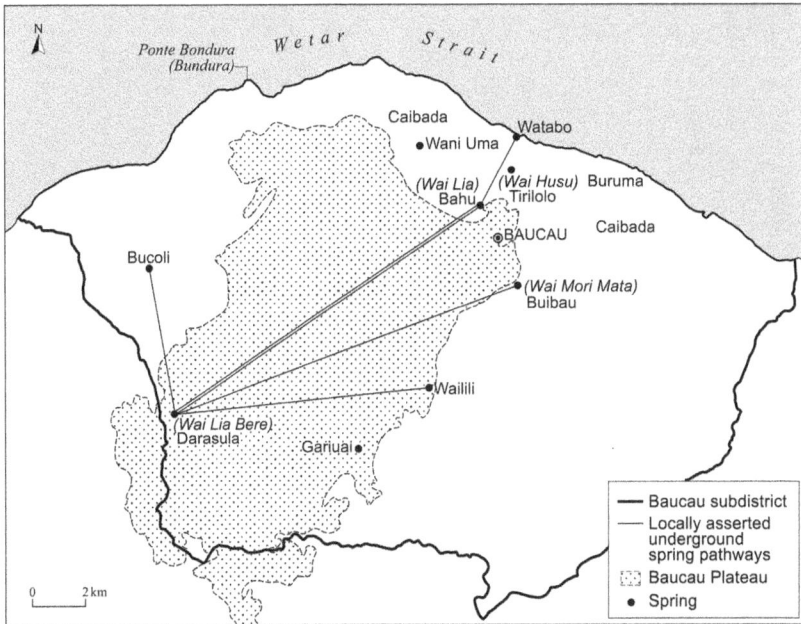

Map 3: Wai Lia Bere's asserted underground flows and spring connections.

Source: Chandra Jayasuriya.

All versions of the story begin by recounting how, one day, there were two brothers up on the plateau tending their buffalo. The brothers were hungry, so they decided to dig, cook and eat some yams. They became thirsty, and then they remembered the day when their dogs went missing nearby and came back to them all wet. They wanted to find out where the dogs got this water, so they made a plan. They cooked some more yams to give to the dogs, but before they gave them the yams they made a bamboo collar—tied with string—for the neck of one of the dogs. Inside the hollow piece of bamboo, they placed ash from the fire and made a small hole. Then they gave them the yams to eat. The dogs soon became thirsty and headed off to look for water. In about one hour they returned, their bodies soaking wet. The brothers followed the ash that had trickled from the bamboo collar until they came to a big cave with water inside. They went down into the cave and drew water, which they carried back out of the cave to drink.

Photo 29: Buffalo and herder on the Baucau plateau.

While the particular details of the subsequent part of the story will vary according to the relationship of the teller's house to these specific underground waters and springs, the water custodians gathered in Baucau that day told the story to the students in the following way. After this, the brothers were still thirsty, so the younger one went down again to fetch water. Inside the cave there were two places from which to draw water. The younger brother could hear the water flowing very loudly from a large opening. He went in to have a look at what was making such a loud noise and suddenly he fell into the water. He was submerged for seven days and seven nights, during which time he encountered two eels, one white and one black. Both eels offered to help him find his way out. He chose to go with the white eel and eventually he emerged in the still water of another cave: Wai Lia in Baucau. If he had instead chosen the black eel, he would have followed the water's underground path to the sea and would never have re-emerged in this world again. During his long journey, he had eaten his clothes as food because the white eel had warned him that if he ate the fruits in the underwater gardens he would never re-emerge. Arriving, naked, in the spring waters of Wai Lia, he decided to stay there and wait beneath the surface.

The story of the white eel always fascinates Russell, the physical geographer who co-teaches the field class with me. 'Of course he went with the white eel,' he tells the students later. Russell explains that eels and other creatures turn translucent when they have been underground for a long period of time, so it makes sense that the younger brother chose to follow the white eel. White eels would know about the underground flows and pathways, while the darker eels would have more recently arrived from waters above ground. Indeed, eels are one of science's most enigmatic species and, while knowledge of their life cycle, travels to freshwater, and spawning and death in the sea is now well known, proof of individual eel movements is much more elusive.

Indeed, science and empirical understandings of the 'natural' world can often only take comparisons with indigenous knowledge so far. A symbolic reading of this story of the white eel flips this analysis entirely. Across Timor, white is synonymous with the sun (the world of the light and the living), while yellow and black are associated with its opposite (the world of darkness and the ancestors). In the Wai Lia eel story, it is in the darkness that true light is to be found.

In the third and final part of this story, the water custodians in Baucau speak of two sisters coming to the spring (the details of the house the sisters belong to will vary according to the storyteller's own house). The older sister entered the cave and drew water. The man from the plateau was crouching beneath the surface and saw the woman drawing water, but he did not move. Then the younger sister came in to draw water. She looked down into the water and beneath it she made out the form of a naked man. He explained: 'I am from the savannah. I was tending buffalo there when I was thirsty and went down into a cave to draw water. Then I somehow ended up here.' 'But what do you want?' asked the women. 'Could you go and ask your brothers to bring me some clothes to wear?' asked the man. So, the women went to ask their older brothers to take the man a *tais* (woven cloth) to wear. They did this, and he got dressed in the water.

Gifting *tais* is, of course, an important part of local marriage exchange. When the man came out of the water, the two sisters and their older brother who had brought the *tais* were still there. It was decided that the younger sister would now marry this man. So, they got married and lived together at the woman's home and they had a child together. Then the woman said, 'It is time for us to go to try to find your place, so I can see where you come from. Do you still have family there, I wonder?' They set off to look for the man's family, telling his story along the way and asking people if they knew of his brother and whether he was still alive. Eventually, they found some of the possessions he had left behind hanging in a tree: his carry basket, cotton-spinning stick, spear and digging stick. He got them down and they kept walking.

By this stage of the story, the couple have crossed the ecotone or transitional zone between two environments: the lush spring groves of the escarpment edge and the much more barren savannah beyond. The ecology of these zones is also reflected in the livelihood differences between the peoples that inhabit them: the people of the coastal springs are irrigated rice growers with large fruit and palm stands, while those on the plateau concentrate on swidden gardens and livestock herding. The distance between the two water sources is only around 25 km, but this was, and is, a substantial cultural journey. The couple kept asking the people they met about the man's brother, and finally one man responded: 'Yes, it is me! I am your older brother. I thought you were lost forever.' The two hugged each other and cried together. The older brother explained that, because the younger brother had returned, they would now make an origin house here by the Wai Lia Bere cave. The house was needed so that offerings could be made to the water below and the story would not be forgotten:

> When the time comes for us to make offerings to give thanks to the water, the people from the villages in Baucau that receive water from Wai Lia must also come together to kill goats, buffalo, pigs and chickens, and then also bring some of them here for us to make our offerings.

'You must also make an origin house at Wai Lia,' said the older brother. This was so the people could also make the same offerings at Wai Lia spring in Baucau.

After this, the brothers made an origin houses in each place, so they could remember this story and give thanks to the water. Each year the local population would carry out ceremonies so that the two water sources would never be dry. This meant that they could make fields, plant rice and have plenty to eat.

Photo 30: *Kabu bee* and rice farmers maintaining the irrigated water channels.

It is this relationship of obligation and reciprocity cemented across the ecotone that lies at the heart of all the various versions of the Wai Lia story. In all versions there is also an important cautionary tale. Eventually, the people from the four villages sharing the water from Wai Lia forgot to make their sacrifices. The water stopped flowing, and many animals, crops and trees began to die. The people from Baucau went to the custodians of the water on the plateau and asked: 'Why is our water dry?' The custodians of the water explained the reason: 'You have not been making the sacrifices and you need to start doing this again.' So, the people in Baucau renewed the required sacrifices and, after this, their rice grew again.

The broader Wai Lia complex in Baucau town is made up of seven interrelated springs that feed the irrigation channels running many kilometres to the rice fields in the east and west of the town. The proper sharing of these irrigation waters is the responsibility of customary water managers known as *kabu bee*. The four villages receiving these waters are in a sibling relationship and are expected to carry out the ceremonies to properly manage the springs. These sacrificial processes—known in Tetum as *fo han* (feeding)—involve small-scale annual sacrifices to ensure that the irrigation waters travel down the constructed water channels to the fields below. They also consist of larger collective seven-yearly ceremonies involving all the water-sharing villages, including those from the plateau, over a period of seven days. In both ceremonies, ritual specialists will call and commune with the sacred eels that inhabit the springs. After each of these events, a portion of the rice harvest will be taken by the *kabu bee* to gift to the custodians of the source waters on the drylands of the plateau. The exchange is something of an agreement: you look after and stay in your place and we will do the same for ours.

Following these watery trails and exchanges across the region since 2006, I slowly came to realise that the Wai Lia stories and those attached to other springs dotted across the wider region are emblematic of the ways in which relationships between people and place in Baucau are configured. Baucau's regional culture is a water culture: one in which caves, springs and their water flows make, connect and bind together (and hold apart) water-sharing communities.

**

In 2018, the origin houses with custodial responsibilities for the Wai Lia spring were somewhat despondent following the recent deaths of two senior elders. One was Major Ko'o Raku, the Makasae-speaking ritual specialist and *lia na'in* (custodian of the words) for Bahu origin village in Baucau. Major Ko'o Raku, a highly revered and sometimes fierce local authority, had first told me his version of the full Wai Lia story in 2008. The other elder who had passed away was a local statesman Joao Baptista, the head of the sub-village of Ana-Ulu and *lia na'in* of the Boilekumu origin house that had custodial responsibilities for the spring complex.

Since the 1960s, Wai Lia had been the town's main water supply and, since independence, the spring had continued to be controlled by the state. As a result, the spring custodians relied on the government's good grace to maintain access to the site and their ceremonial responsibilities. Three years earlier, they had collected money from the citizenry of the various villages to carry out a large-scale community water-sharing ceremony at Wai Lia. This ceremony hadn't been performed for many years, and the complex negotiations to enable it were taking time. The loss of the main ritual leader and senior custodian had further complicated arrangements. Mari Kai Wai Mata Bu, the custodian whose ancestor had travelled underground from the plateau and emerged in Wai Lia, described the problem as a relative imbalance of power. 'We are only the small people. We must wait for the government,' he said.

Mari Kai didn't volunteer further explanation for the delay and major sticking point—it was understood that the government was expected to contribute substantial resources to the ceremony. As a major user and beneficiary of the spring, government would be expected to contribute the 'big sacrificial blood'—the buffalo—to enable the waters to flow. Whether the state is willing to assume these long-term ritual responsibilities to the ancestors remains something of an open question.

We were joined in our discussion by Fernando, the son of the recently deceased senior custodian and something of an introvert. Speaking hesitantly at first, he seemed to defer to Mari Kai Wai Mata Bu. But, as he spoke his confidence increased, and I could hear the voice of his father, Joao. Fernando was clearly growing in his authority and capacity to speak. He was beginning to own the story and take on the customary leadership role of his father.

Photo 31: Wai Lia spring pool and government pump station.

I was especially pleased this year that we had continued to allocate time in our itinerary for this encounter. Because of the way it is designed, the field class needs to cover a lot of geographic territory (over very bad roads) in a short space of time. The visit to Baucau is really a lunch stop on a much longer journey. Yet, each year, the water custodians are especially keen to talk with the students and host a visit to the spring. After we speak with them in the restaurant, the entire class follows them through the main part of town on a walk around and through the Wai Lia spring site. The walk ends with the group convening by the main water pool inside the government's water supply station. The sight of the water custodians gathered at this site with a large group of eager young foreigners in tow sends a potent and tangible reminder to the state of their caretaker responsibilities—both to the spring complex and the range of human and non-human beings who continue to nurture their varied custodial roles within it.

On this occasion, Fernando finished by telling us about the increasingly poor state of the irrigated rice fields that used to cascade down from Wai Lia's lush groves to the coastal plains below. He said that many of these rice fields, including those of his own family, were now abandoned due to lack of water. The government was redirecting the agricultural flow away from the irrigation channels and into the piped water supply for the burgeoning post-independence town.

I heard a similar account from a local teacher who told me, sadly, that her family's rice fields were also abandoned. She, however, squarely attributed the blame to the decline of the town's customary water management practices. 'They haven't been doing the appropriate ceremonies at the spring,' she said. Her reasoning was that the custodians (*bee na'in*) and the customary managers of the water (the *kabu bee*) had not taken the required tributes to the water's source on the plateau. 'That's the reason the water's not flowing. It's not flowing to either the spring or to the rice fields.'

Wherever the blame lay, the various accounts all agreed that the government needed to come together with the appropriate spring custodians, ritual leaders, customary water managers and village heads to work out a resolution. While they had long been keen for the government to step up its brokering role, the spring custodians also made it clear that they needed some time to recover from the loss of their elders, and to renew and, where necessary, realign their own relationships.

***

Another water-related problem in Baucau was the current state of village politics. Across all four villages and associated sub-villages comprising the old town, many senior leaders had recently died or been replaced in village elections. In many cases, they had been replaced by a much younger generation of educated men (more rarely, women). Some of these men are the sons or grandsons of earlier generations of village leaders. While the village-level of administration is subject to democratic elections, the successful candidates will often be the descendants of previous leaders. Unlike their forebears, these men usually have the literacy to navigate the modern bureaucracy. However, they do not necessarily have the knowledge of how to activate customary governance processes. Many do not even know their own constituencies well.

One day I was visiting my friend and long-term research collaborator Jose da Costa at his home just below Baucau's old town in an area known colloquially as *abut laran* (literally: inside the roots). Jose is a both a *kabu bee* (keeper of the water) and local healer of all kinds of human ailments. We sat on his hillside veranda among the shade of breadfruit trees and gazed out across the tops of coconut palms to the coastline below. Our conversation was punctuated that day by two things: the normal and incessant crowing of Jose's many fighting cockerels, and a certain sadness that I thought I could detect slipping into the demeanour of a man whose life practices are under threat. Jose, his wife and I sat together and slowly sipped the cool drinks he had sent one of his grandchildren to purchase in honour of our visit. 'The new generation don't know the stories, the histories and how we are all bound together,' they lamented. Connected to those stories are agricultural practices that underpin both local livelihoods and continuously build community. As the water supply for the irrigation channels continued to diminish year by year, the rice fields lay increasingly vacant below the old town. Both of them were also feeling an absence in the practical bonds that held together their community. Another longstanding concern for Jose and other water custodians and customary leaders from the wider Baucau area was government plans to support the construction of a local cement factory and mine. Since 2014, sections of so-called barren lands (comprising Cape Bondura to the west and nearby areas of the plateau inland from Baucau) had been earmarked for limestone mining. While the local village heads and political leaders of the Baucau new town and plateau area were reported to have given their support for the stage one mine and factory site development, at the time the origin clans with acknowledged ritual authority over Cape Bondura had not been properly engaged nor consulted.

The proposal, developed in late 2013 and brokered by national level politicians and bureaucrats, included plans to mine the local limestone for the next 100 years with the promise of hundreds of local jobs and economic development. While many in the broader community welcomed the initiative, others were apprehensive. Some voiced concerns that the removal of rock from coastal areas would result in the sea rising up to swallow all the agricultural land. Others were worried about movement of the *talibere* (python), a spirit being connected to Cape Bondura and understood to enable the flow of underground waters. Some from the plateau area feared that the quarrying would also disturb spirit beings associated with their water sources and cause the karstic waters to dry up.

It was in this context that a local community group from Cape Bondura called Kapeliwa was established in 2014 'to protect and preserve the Waima'a [speaking] communities' rights to their culture, development and traditional land rights'.[1] But, despite their initial demands, the group's campaign for greater consultation and information about the cement mine proposal, publicised through a 'global voices' network of NGOs, did not progress. Indigenous activism of the kind connected to a pan-indigenous global movement is not something that people in Baucau are familiar with. Their struggles are much more localised and introspective.

Many other people in the wider Baucau area welcomed the economic boom heralded by the proposed development. Indeed, many saw prosperity as their due, a rightful independence dividend paid out by the government in the form of special economic zones like ZEESM in Oecusse and the planned south coast oil and gas production corridor. Those with the means to do so had purchased haulage trucks from Indonesia in anticipation of a concrete-driven sub-contracting boom. The slogan 'Your Dream, We Build It' was splashed across the banner of the Timor-Leste Cement Company's website. However, despite the public campaign falling silent, others continued to whisper private concerns that the rightful owners or ritual custodians of the land had not yet given their permission for the development.

---

1   Sara Moreira. 'East Timorese Protect Land Rights Against Australian Cement Plant Deal'. *Global Voices*, 21 April 2014, accessed 28 February 2016, globalvoices.org/2014/04/21/east-timor-land-rights-australia-cement-plant-deal/.

On New Year's Day in January 2017, an event occurred that rattled many nerves. At the coastal site demarcated for the cement factory's construction, in an area made accessible by a road newly prepared for the mine, a visitor disappeared while swimming. For several days there was no trace of the swimmer and rumours circulated that he had been taken by the *avo* (a word with the dual meaning of grandparent and estuarine crocodile). The authorities instigated a search, but it was not until a representative of the land custodial group went down to the seashore to carry out a ritual invocation to the ancestors of the sea that the body was recovered. Once the custodian requested that the body of the unfortunate swimmer be returned to the shore, the dismembered corpse washed up on the beach within a day.

The death shocked the community who shared gruesome images of the deceased on their phones, and much discussion ensued about the increasing incidence of crocodile attacks. In the past, these attacks had been considered to be very rare. Without publicly saying so, the community wondered why the *avo* were apparently turning against their people. For some, the answer was worryingly clear: these *avo*, powerful beings of the sea and local cosmology, were angry at the development plans for the cement mine and this death was their warning. Unchecked by customary processes, an angered *lulik* could wreak devastation on all.

In 2018, I heard conflicting anecdotes about progress of the cement mine. The new road was now in active use and new houses had been built along the road leading up to the cape. However, it seemed that the company's storage containers had been removed from the site. Nevertheless, a woman who had opened a coastal fish restaurant by the side of the new road told me in no uncertain terms that the factory was going ahead as planned. And still I heard from others that the land custodians were refusing to give permission for the development. My sister-in-law, who was active in the newly formed local tourism association, also expressed concerns about the mine. Extremely optimistically I thought, she considered that the area opened by the new road might be better used for development of a luxury resort.

One day, I met up with an old friend, Amau, who had been involved in setting up training centres connected to national development initiatives. He was disappointed at the lack of progress on the mine. Along with many Timorese, he shared the government's vision for the establishment of flourishing regional economies, wherein increasingly skilled workers were enabled to take up jobs and contribute to the improved living conditions set out in the country's national strategic development plan for 2011–30.

But my friend was conflicted. From the perspective of one who also had customary ritual obligations for one of the springs that may be affected by the mine, he was circumspect and had concerns about the project. Referencing previous work together on the spring water research, he said: 'Everything we went and saw could be gone.' I was surprised by his sudden and frank admission, but I realised that this is the dilemma for many local people. People across the region hold aspirations for development, but they must balance them with deep concerns about the environmental and cultural costs. According to the sketchy mining development plans Amau had seen, the caves, water sources, trees and vegetation would disappear. 'What will the company replace it with?' he asked. 'What will happen to the underground water flows?' As the government had not publicly released the expert impact assessment reports enquiring into the effects of the proposal, people had only verbal guarantees from the company and the government that the development would be okay. But even those who supported the development in principle worried about the possible consequences.

***

Towards the end of our time in Baucau, we visited old friends in the villages closer to Cape Bondura. Discussions inevitably turned to the mine development. The daughter of one local leader told us that she and her father supported the mine. 'We want development,' she said, adding that, while she couldn't wait for the development to proceed, her father's younger brother was opposed to the mine. A young local leader from another village, who had assumed the mantle from his father, told us that the people from his area, and the other custodial clans of the lands of Cape Bondura itself, had not been involved in the formal decision-making. 'We have been left outside it,' he said. Those who wanted it to go ahead were the more recent newcomers to the area with lesser claims to the land. In the event that the mine proceeded, the custodial clans had agreed among themselves that they would not take jobs with the company. 'Let them [the others] go ahead. We will see what happens,' he said. He explained that those making the decisions were from newcomer groups who originated from areas of Baucau's old town five generations ago.

> The custodians of the Cape welcomed them and said they could use the land, but it was understood they had only use rights. But now they are acting as if they are the owners of the land.

The young man added that the village head from the cape (a vocal mine development supporter) had become very ill and was now housebound. The cause of this illness was left hanging in the air.

I asked this young leader about something I had been puzzling over for a while. Why had the recognised custodian clans of the cape been silent on this issue in the Timorese media? 'They can't say much either way,' said my friend. He explained quietly how this was a complicated problem of relationships and rights and how the elders who speak for that area had yet to speak. 'They have yet to say yes or no. No one has even properly asked them.' Because of their initial exclusion from negotiations and the absence of what they saw as proper customary processes, the elders had given the responsibility to publicly respond to the development over to *lulik*. 'So now, the living can't speak, they can't get involved. It's up to *lulik*.'

8

Ritual and Recovery

While in Baucau, our friend Atinu invited us to participate in a healing ceremony at Wai Lia Bere, the famous cave water source on an otherwise arid plateau. I had worked with Atinu as a research collaborator and translator over many years. His father, who had been an important figure in my early water research, had died a few years earlier, and Atinu had then become the senior custodian of Wai Lia Bere and its associated house, Ledatame Ikun. My participation in this event was encouraged by Atinu, and together we were making a film on customary approaches to healing. While the footage of this day was not, in the end, included in the final film, the event had a profound influence on the film's composition.

As I understood it, one of Atinu's nephews was ill and was going to be healed by the waters flowing beneath the Wai Lia Bere cave. It turned out, though, that I had misunderstood the gist of the story. This was not exactly a healing ceremony: Atinu's nephew had been very ill and had almost died, but he was already healed. Something had attacked him and taken his spirit. But with the water's help, the family had recovered it, and his spirit had been restored to his body. Now was the time to acknowledge and formally thank these healing ancestral waters. The purpose of the ceremony was to give thanks to the ancestral spirits for his return to health.

Wai Lia Bere is said to feed the flow of water to Wai Lia in Baucau and it is the cave through which the younger of the buffalo-herding brothers had long ago travelled after their dog had located the water source. This cave is also understood to be a gateway or 'door' for water flowing to other springs in the region; it is considered a critical feeder of springs across the escarpment zone. I had first visited Wai Lia Bere eight years ago for a community ceremony aimed at ensuring this downstream flow of water. It seemed that my research had come full circle. Back then, I was just beginning my journey to understand this complex watery landscape. Now I was back again, only now I was focused on research into Timorese approaches to healing.

Despite the fact I hadn't met with most of the senior men during an interlude of eight years, we were now greeted like old friends. Some things had changed. We remembered Atinu's father and another senior ritual leader, now gone. Eight years ago I had met Atinu, but this was the first day I had met his wife, Silvana. She had had her own struggle with illness over the years and had lived much of the intervening time in her natal house in the mountains of Matebian. She and Atinu had suffered greatly, losing a child during that period. Yet, today, as we gathered at their house prior to heading to Wai Lia Bere, she was proudly serving her visitors coffee and fried bananas, and Atinu sat happily holding their nine-month-old baby, Olivia. At the time of our first meeting eight years ago, he had been working as a teacher, and everyone still refers to him in this role. But, having trained as a veterinarian during the Indonesian era, he now worked in the Ministry of Agriculture. With his deep understanding of local languages and cultures, Atinu is a man adept at working across worlds.

When we had first met in 2008 it was only a brief encounter. I had already met, and was familiar with, his father, his brother and a cousin. Yet Atinu had made an impression on me; he was quiet and understated but clearly attentive to the aims of the water research. It was not, however, until my father-in-law's favourite dog, Lobu, needed urgent veterinary attention that we again sought him out. Private vets are unheard of in Baucau, but as we now knew about Atinu's role treating livestock for the agriculture department, we took a chance and drove up to his rental house in town. Atinu did not think our request strange and responded with a house call, attending to the dog with great care and concern. With Lobu healed, our connection with Atinu had also been deepened. Dogs feature in many of the region's water stories, creating bonds between people and communities over long distances. While veterinary care was a twist on this tradition, as Atinu himself reminded us, dogs are *lulik* for his Ledatame Ikun house; they are effectively its life-givers. We later discovered that Atinu was also related to us through marriage as his mother's family were in a longstanding relationship as the life-giving house for Quin's grandmother's house.

Wai Lia Bere is a part of the Makasae-speaking village of Gariuai, but it is located on the savannah in the Gariuai sub-village of Darasula (the name translates as 'the edge of the savannah') (see Map 3 in Chapter 7). The former *chefe* (head) of Darasula was there at Atinu's house, too. Although no longer formally the sub-village head, he is still referred to as *chefe*. He lives down and on the other side of the road from Atinu. This slight difference in east–west geography means that the *chefe* will usually speak Waima'a at home. Meanwhile, the households on Atinu's side of the road usually speak Makasae. Atinu and the *chefe* are first cousins and they are adept speakers of both languages, yet this modern road marks a much older border. A savannah-edge meeting point between cultural groups has been preserved to this day linguistically, if not in the village administrative structures.

While waiting for the others to arrive, the *chefe* told me he has frequently re-watched the short video of the water-increase ceremony that I had made for him and other villagers eight years ago. He said that watching it makes him feel closer to those who are no longer living. Sitting next to the *chefe* was Simiao, his cousin's (and Atinu's sister's) son. Simiao, who studies at university in Dili, shyly brought out his smart phone to show us photos of himself when he was ill. His whole body was swollen, but especially his arms. He couldn't walk or move his arms for many weeks and moved back to Darasula to be cared for by his family. He thought he was going to die. He explained, though, that this wasn't a medical problem. While nurses from Baucau would sometimes come and give him injections to help with the swelling, afterwards the swelling would increase. So the nurses said that he needed to wait for the swelling to settle before they could treat him again. Simiao explained that the nurses told Simiao's family that they 'must first look for the source of the problem inside your own house'. This meant asking the ancestors. Simiao's maternal uncles began a quest to locate the source of the problem. To do this, they sacrificed a chicken and examined its liver for signs of ancestral displeasure. 'It tells them what the problems are,' Simiao explained.

> Later, after we knew the source of the problem, I was healed by medicine from his mother's house. Today, we are paying the debt to the ancestors for enabling that healing. I was ill because my father's house wasn't in order and that left me open to attack from dangerous spirits. I have been good for about a month now.

The *chefe* also explained to me how Atinu and another senior ritual leader had come together at the Ledatame Ikun house to find a way to restore Simiao's health. After a complicated fact-finding mission, they had carried out a ritual to seek help from the ancestors of the house—the same house whose ancestor had travelled underground from the Wai Lia Bere cave and emerged at the Wai Lia spring in Baucau all those generations ago. The cure was achieved through a two-step process: access to waters of Wai Lia Bere, followed by a ritual to sacralise betel leaves inside the Ledatame Ikun, his mother's and uncles' houses. These leaves were then taken by Atinu and rubbed over the body of the seriously ill Simiao. We were going to Wai Lia Bere to give thanks to the ancestral spirits of the water. The following day a similar ritual would take place at the Ledatame Ikun house.

By now, around 20 men had gathered at the house, our departure point. The first man sped off with a goat and lengths of cut bamboo tied up in the back of this three-wheel motorbike. Others departed on two-wheel motorbikes with chickens bound to the handlebars and various numbers of pillion passengers on the back. Others of us piled into our four-wheel-drive vehicle. We were all headed several kilometres inland along a dusty open-savannah track to Wai Lia Bere.

Photo 32: Main road, Darasula.

By the time our car arrived at the scrubby clearing near the entry to Wai Lia Bere cave, the ceremony preparations were in full swing. The chickens had been assembled by the tree and rock altar, along with the goat. The bamboo was being cut up further for cooking and for use as water receptacles. Strings of areca palm nut were hung by a senior ritual leader on a notch on the tree. An old man was laying out baskets of betel leaf and lime powder on the stone altar. Lastly, he added a packet of cigarettes. Counting seven chickens in total, I surmised it to be a significant ceremony.

Much later, I found out that offerings relating to Simiao's sickness and healing was only one of a suite of offerings that day. The healing was being directed at both the individual and at the broader collective who were gathered at the spring. This dual purpose was abundantly clear to everyone else, but it hadn't been explained to us. The ceremony was carried out in Makasae, and sometimes Waima'a. While Quin speaks some Makasae, he is not from the area nor an expert on the deeper functioning of the ritual world. At these events, he often prefers to remain in the background and talk politics with the younger men. Luckily, I had been to enough similar ceremonies of this general kind to be able to follow and anticipate the flow of events. Managing the boredom and demands of our kids during such an event was another matter, but even they were getting used it.

Mari Kai Wai Mata Bu (literally meaning 'Mari Kai the owner of the water'), a direct descendant of the ancestor who had fallen into the cave waters, travelled underground and emerged in the Wai Lia spring in Baucau, was present at the ceremony and would have a major role in each of the ritual stages. At one point early on, I noticed one of the senior men snip off a piece of the goat's ear, seemingly without the notice of the goat, and walk off in another direction with two of the chickens. I was told that he was going to make offerings to Wai Mata Ana, another deep cave and water source nearby that is sometimes referred to as the 'wife' to Wai Lia Bere. It is from this cave, some Baucau people tell me, that Wai Lia Bere water custodians are able to manipulate the water supply to those lower down in the watershed.

Once again, I was filming the ceremony. Afterwards I would edit it and it would be given to those present on the day. As well as being a contribution to the film we were making, the video process is also for me a research tool. I simply can't observe and take everything in at these complex events. Video allows me to observe and take in a range of other sensory experiences, while creating a detailed visual record. This record means I can later sit with the process again, notice details that escaped me at the time and try to make sense of the whole. It is always important to pay attention to exactly who was doing what, how and when. As most of the ceremony was in Makasae, I could call on Quin to help me later translate the gist of what is being said. Even so, I know that much will remain opaque. To dwell deeper in the ritual politics and processes at play I would need to sit, for many more hours, with Atinu. Together we would need to work through the translation into Tetum and discuss at length the various possible interpretations of what was being said and done.

After the senior man had taken the goat's ear and chickens to Wai Mata Ana, the next two stages of the ritual involved separate offerings of the goat and a black chicken at Wai Lia Bere. While the chicken was taken directly to the entrance of the cave, the body of the much larger goat was absent, but it was made present through prayer. Later, a twig collected from the rock and tree altar at the cave's entrance was brushed over the head of the goat when the animal was sacrificed at the savannah altar. Following the chicken and goat sacrifices, each animal's liver or entrails would be read by the assembled senior ritual experts, and the body parts cooked by the youth. In this way, the ancestors are speaking through and with the bodies of these animals. After this, all of the cooked body parts would be laid out as offerings by the altar for the final ceremony.

Only the senior ritual leaders made journeys to the cave entrance, and I followed them with my video camera. All of the others stayed by the savannah altar, seamlessly engaged in the many tasks of food preparation. Apart from Madalena and myself, all roles were performed by men and boys on this occasion. When I asked if women were ordinarily prohibited at such ceremonies, the *chefe* simply said that the women were all busy. With so much to do on the home front, they couldn't always get away for ceremonies. This casual division of labour reminded me that food preparation in Timor is by no means the sole task of women.

During the first prayer by the cave entrance, the two ritual leaders squatted on the ground in front of the simple rock altar. Mari Kai Wai Mata Bu stood behind them. One of the old men began to speak to the ancestors of the cave:

We are making this offering to you of a goat and a male and female chicken. This is our final offering in this process. We are small people, you are big. Please look after us. Don't be angry or jealous. We have offered this to you. Protect us, too, from getting sick when others who might be angry or jealous of us seek to do us harm. We are looking to you for protection. Please look after us. Look after those of us who are not here. Look after those who are away studying. Help them write well.

During the second offering, we returned to the entrance with a single black chicken. We were accompanied by a man from Cape Bondura. He squatted behind the two old ritual leaders, one of whom held the chicken. Mari Kai stood once more at the rear. The old man holding the chicken began again to speak to the ancestors:

Now, in the era of democracy, many of your people are studying far away from here. Some travel over the sea. They work with pens. Please look after them. Keep them safe. Help them to do their jobs well. This is their offering to you.

The next stage of the ceremony occurred back at the savannah altar. Simiao and his father were called to sit in front of the altar. Holding the red rooster, one of the ritual leaders spoke to the ancestors:

Your grandson has brought a chicken to thank you for healing his sickness. He has brought a chicken, so we can call out and honour your name. Something attacked him, but you helped him. Please don't make him sick again. We as elders are speaking, we are praying for him. Not all our in-law houses could come, but your grandson's father speaks for them. His words will reach you.

Squatting down in front of the altar, the father spoke humbly, eyes to the ground. He repeated a similar message, only this time his words were spoken in Waima'a. He gave thanks to the ancestral owners of the land and waters for healing his son. The rooster was then killed, and its liver was read. Much consternation and discussion accompanied the reading. Later, I was told that the reading had revealed that others from outside the Wai Lia Bere custodial house, Ledatame, were still jealous and that they were still making 'bad medicine'. 'What will you do?' I asked Simiao's father. Looking at me a little incredulously he replied: 'The ancestors will look after us now. We have given the issue to them.'

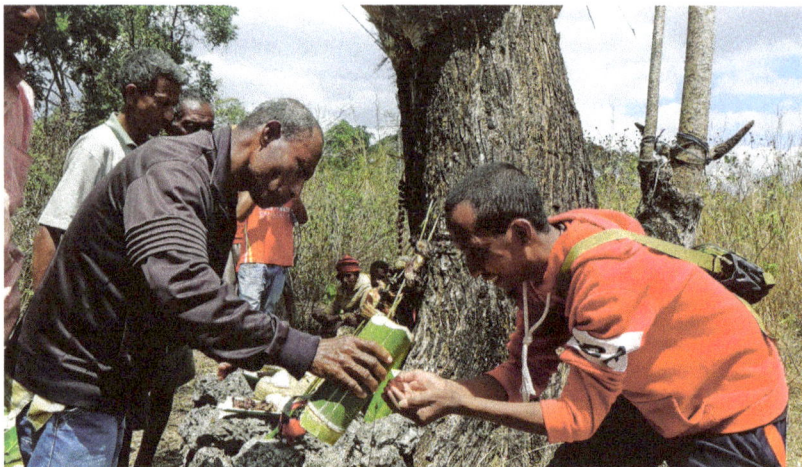

Photo 33: Simiao and final water blessing.

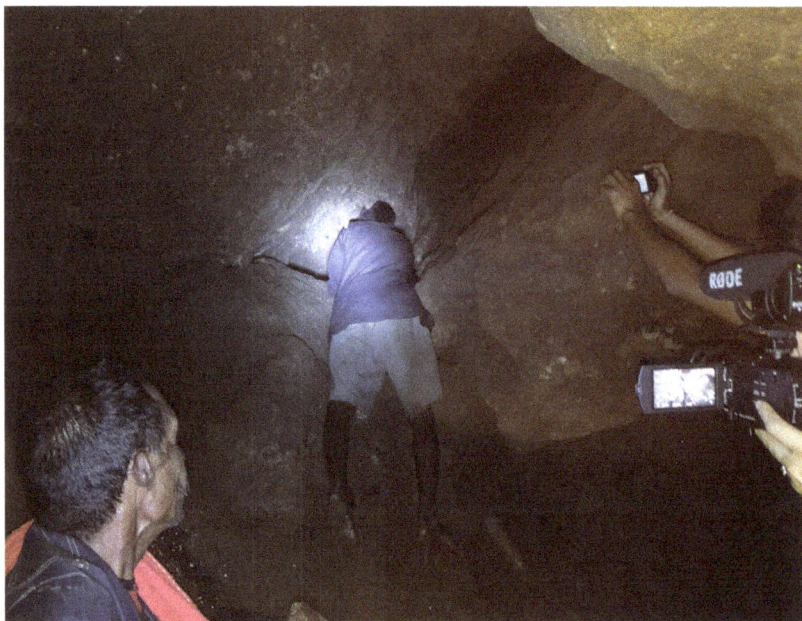

Photo 34: Offering inside Wai Lia Bere cave.

After all the animals had been offered, read and prepared, and the new rice had been cooked in the bamboo lengths, all the food was laid out on bamboo plates—on the altar for the ancestors, and on the ground for the living. It was then time to take an offering down a narrow and steep pathway, into the cave itself. We descended about 10 metres underground before we reached the water. A bamboo plate of meat and rice was placed by one of the ritual leaders on a rocky upper ledge above the water. Mari Kai and others used flashlights on their phones to scramble down the rocks and fill their jerry cans from the fast-flowing stream of water that rushed through the cave. This was the place where Mari Kai's ancestor had fallen all those years ago. 'Go carefully,' others yelled out from above, lest history repeat itself.

After drawing water, we returned to the savannah altar for the penultimate stage of the ceremony. Water was poured into bamboo lengths and placed on the altar. Mari Kai would use this water later to wash the bodies of the cured Simiao and his close associates. All of those connected to the Ledatame Ikun house and the houses of its significant in-laws were now seated or squatting in front of the altar. I noticed for the first time a yellow dog that sat majestically among them. The senior ritual leaders took turns speaking to the ancestors. The first man spoke:

> We can't be jealous or angry. We are the small people. Our elders have died. Only we are left, the small people. You need to look after us, to help us fix things, to follow the path. We don't know the details of what our ancestors did and promised each other. But as in the past, we continue making our offerings to you. We will always call out and honour your name.

Then, a second ritual leader took over:

> I am your grandparent's child. There have been problems, but we have all come together to fix them. We have resolved it. We have told everyone. We seek your forgiveness. We [the living] have resolved our problems. Now you need to look after us. Give us life.

> We ask you, our ancestors and our future generations, don't make us sick. We are the small people; our elders have gone. We have come together, both sides of these family alliances. If there was conflict in the past, we don't know the details. Please give us pardon.

> You know it all, but please forgive us our ignorance. Pass on your spirit to us. Give us your force. Reinforce these offerings we have made to all the ancestors.

> We [the living] will always be family together. We are Wai Husu Wai Lewa. We are small, but together. We ask our children not to cause problems among the living.

Why, I wondered, did this last prayer refer to Wai Husu Wai Lewa? I knew, from previous research, that the ritually paired springs of Wai Husu Wai Lewa referred to the powerful alliance that brought villages together from across the lush Baucau escarpment zone and its drier hinterland. The leader was drawing on an ancestral pact and governance arrangement intended to ensure peace, harmony and water sharing across the region. Yet here the alliance was being invoked in relation to the healing ceremony of this 20-something young man whose life, it was now clear, had hung in the balance because of unfinished business in the ancestral past.

Later, when all the ceremony was done, Atinu organised for his nephew, Simiao's father and the *chefe* to explain, for the purposes of the video, what had gone on during the ritual and the background to these events. The *chefe* explained how the ceremony was tied to 'an ancient path', a longstanding connection between particular origin houses:

> This is our riches. Our riches come from strengthening these relations to strengthen our health. If we leave behind this heritage, we are in trouble. Our ancestors give us our health. We can't lose this tradition. This is our Timorese identity.

Simiao told me later, after the ceremony: 'Today I feel proud. When I was sick the whole family gathered together to enable me to regain my health. If they hadn't come together, I might have died.' For Simiao and his family, family unity was the key to healing:

> If the family doesn't come together when there are problems we can't live well. In the past our ancestors were together. We need to be together too. For us, health and culture go together. Going on our own doesn't work. Both sides of the family must come together.

Atinu had told me that he wouldn't say much during the interview. But, as usual, it was his interview—the final statement of the day—that offered the greatest clarity. He told me how, as members of the house of Ledatame Ikun, his family were connected to the story of the water of Wai Lia, the spring in Baucau. It was their ancestor who travelled through the water and that was why it was important that Mari Kai Wai Mata Bu was also present at the ceremony. He explained: 'We don't carry out our curing rituals with things other than water and betel leaf.' As his in-laws and nephew had been attacked by an angered spirit, betel leaves taken from the Ledatame house were needed to repel the attack.

> We needed to use two bundles of five and seven leaves. Five of them were for the ancestors of the house; the bundle of seven were for our ancestors that now reside in the water. We used this to cure our nephew. Now he is better.

The power of the Wai Lia underground water was thus central to the healing process. It is the water that gives the power to the senior ritual leaders of Ledatame Ikun to heal. Just as the politics of water sharing permeates the lives of those living in the lower part of the watershed, so it permeates life up on the plateau.

Atinu explained that, to repay the debt to these ancestors, two ceremonies were needed: one at the cave to repay the debt to the powerful ancestors and nature spirits that gave the house its security, and a second ceremony at the Ledatame Ikunhouse, involving a further goat and two chickens. The latter would take place the next day 'to tell the ancestors of the house that it was through their culture that we were able to bring this boy back from the dead'.

According to Atinu, the cause of the sickness was a break in the marital pathway of exchanges flowing between the intermarried houses of Ledatame Ikun and Gariuai:

> We needed to get things in order. This is why we brought everyone together today at Wai Lia Bere. We informed the ancestors of the success of the healing. As a result, we have all recovered *matak malirin* [greening coolness], our capacity to flourish in life.

The path flowing between the houses of Ledatame Ikun and Gariuai was a transgenerational one:

> Generations ago, we gave them a place here in the savannah to live. Until this day, if they encounter problems or sickness, they will come to the house of Ledatame Ikun to restore their capacity to flourish.

Photo 35: Simiao's father at medicinal tree.

Simiao's father's house, where our interview took place, is not far from the underground waters of Wai Lia Bere. The nearby land was used to grow an acre or so of chilli and tomato, both of which relied on groundwater. While the crops belonged to the household, the farming is taking place on the land of Ledatame Ikun. The land and the water are conjoined in a land use arrangement that extends generations into the past. The power of the water infuses with the land. When we arrived at the house, Simiao's father grabbed a crowbar and signalled for us to follow him behind the house and into the savannah. He took us a short distance to a spindly 2-metre-tall tree, where he kneeled down and carefully dug away some of the red earth to expose the tree's roots. 'I dug up some of this root,' he said with great pride. 'It also helped cure my son and enabled him to recover from the attack.'

The eventual film *Holding Tightly: Custom and Healing in Timor-Leste*[1] observes various manifestations of *hun no dikin*, the key Timorese botanical metaphor that in Tetum translates literally as 'base/trunk and

---

1   See: *Holding Tightly: Custom and Healing in Timor-Leste*, Ronin Films, Arkivu Dijitál Kultura no Ekolojia Timor-Leste (Cultural Ecology of Timor-Leste Digital Archive), 2021, accessed 25 June 2021, arkivukulturaekolojia.com/waimata-films#/films-holding-tightly/.

tips', more symbolically as 'beginnings and endings/renewal'. This core image of the tree, roots and sprouting tips reflects intertwined human and non-human relationships and processes. Botanical life cycles of watering, growth, flowering, decline and regeneration reflect these human and non-human growth pathways, the connections between houses, their roots or base and their tips or new generations. The metaphor leads on directly to another: *matak malirin* (greening coolness), the aim of all ritual processes concerning life flourishing, good health and vitality. As Jose da Costa, the healer and keeper of the water from Baucau town, once told me: 'Water cures people. The power of water comes from its coolness. All medicine gets its life from water.'

9

Life in the Rice Fields

Quin was always telling the kids and me about how he spent much of his early childhood in his grandmother's village of Bercoli, a small rural Waima'a-speaking village in the foothills of the central ranges about 40 minutes south of Baucau town. Like Baucau, it features dryland savannah in its upper reaches and spring-fed groves and rice terraces in its lower reaches. His memories of the rice planting and harvest seasons are of long periods spent working in the fields with extended family members, of the paddy being trampled by buffalo and horses, and of lots of adventures slingshotting birds for meaty snacks. During the harvest, the days would merge with nights spent out in the rice houses, threshing the rice stalks by foot in large family groups. It is never the hard labour that Quin remarks on. Rather, he recounts the nights spent dancing, singing and telling stories to accompany the work of threshing, the sleeping out together in the rice houses and the rice field meals prepared by his aunties. Quin wanted Madalena and Zeca to experience that life, too.

By the time of our arrival in May, the rice harvest was in full swing. The rains had been good in February and March, but they had disappeared in April and most of the rain-fed rice fields had withered. Meanwhile, the rice fed by springs was doing relatively well. The valley had transitioned from verdant green to a thick golden carpet. People were expecting a good harvest. On the day we reached Bercoli, no one was home: they were all down in the lower fields in the valley. As we walked from the road down through the already harvested sections of the fields, we noticed many bamboo lengths leaning on rocks and tiny fireplaces in the corners of the fields. Each of these offerings signalled that the ceremonies had been carried out to seek ancestral permission for the harvest of the particular field. In the areas where the harvest was complete, more elaborate ritual signs signalled another set of rituals was complete.

Photo 36: Rice harvest ritual offering.

Every rice field area—referred to as an *ulu* (head)—has its own history associated with ancestors and ceremonies. While the repertoire of ceremonies is broadly similar, the ancestral invocations attached to each area vary. The first ceremony required is the pre-harvest ceremony. In the Bercoli valley, this involves a chicken, eggs and a portion of the previous year's rice offered in bamboo lengths to the custodians, the ancestors of the fields and the springs that water the fields. Another ceremony must be carried out prior to the rice being carried home. The final ceremony of the harvest period is the *saur haree* (new rice consecration ceremony), in which rice is first offered to the ancestors at the origin house site in exchange for blessings on the health of all those involved in the harvest and for prosperity in the coming agricultural year. Until this ceremony is complete, the senior representatives of each house may not consume the new rice.

We made our way down the slippery, mud-filled paths between the rice terraces to find Quin's uncles and male cousins busily threshing their newly harvested rice. In the rice house next to the field, a woman was cooking rice and stew for the workers. Quin's cousin Noyti and her neighbour Luciana worked nearby and had nearly finished harvesting an area that belonged to other family members. Noyti and Luciana are sharecroppers in another area of rice across the valley. These fields, in a stunning location just below the main springs of Wai Daba and Ocabai and facing the mountains of Matebian, had been bequeathed to Noyti by her father. The women told us that their fields would not be ready for harvest for another month and so we promised to come back to help them with the harvest. Unlike in Atambua, where contract labour is now predominantly used for the rice planting and harvest, in Bercoli most rice is produced for family consumption and the rice is harvested by family and neighbourhood groupings.

Before leaving, we shared lunch with the women in the rice house. The food was good, but the rice was not as nutty and tasty as I remembered from past visits to the village. The reddish-brown tinge of the bran was notably absent from the grain. Noyti and Luciana concurred about the reduced quality and taste of the local rice. Even just a few years ago, locally produced rice was more flavoursome and, when consumed with local vegetables and chilli or simply as a rice porridge, each mouthful was like a vitamin hit. Now, if the rice is cooked over an open fire, some of this flavour is retained, but the rice varieties and growing practices themselves have changed.

Photo 37: Wai Daba rice fields with Mt Ariana in background (Old Man at right).

The Timorese government and donor agencies have worked hard to introduce new improved, higher yielding and longer lasting seed varieties that have been distributed across the country for free. But increased productivity seems to have come at the cost of flavour and the nutritional value of the grains. With the increased use of mechanised rice husking in the final stage of grain preparation, the bran of the rice is completely polished away, further reducing taste and nutrients. This is especially noticeable in lean times, when a meal may consist only of rice and a chilli salsa. In the past, even this was filling and delicious.

While recognising that the new varieties and processes save labour time and obtain higher yields, Noyti and Luciana lamented the changes. They pointed out that younger generations of Timorese no longer know how to select, and save, the diversity of seeds once tailored by farmers for local agricultural production. Nor do younger generations know as much about the stages needed to properly dry out the grains in the sun or how to husk the rice by hand. In many cases, younger urban Timorese do not even know how to clean and prepare rice for cooking. 'There is no going back,' Noyti and Luciana said.

★★★

Two weeks later, we returned to Bercoli to help out with the remainder of the harvest. Noyti's fields were still not ready, so we began work in the lower fields, an area we soon understood as the centre of power in the valley. This area, known as Kai Bo'o, contained fields shared between the siblings of Quin's uncle and Noyti's father, Elisio. He is the senior ritual leader for the valley and the senior customary law man for the entire village, frequently consulted on issues arising in both its savannah and valley environments. In Kai Bo'o, most of the siblings had already harvested their rice and completed their ceremonies required to carry it home. Yet all of their rice was still stored out in the fields. Before their rice could be taken home, cultural injunctions require that they must wait for Tiu Elisio's rice harvest and for the completion of his ceremonies.

Tiu Elisio—often referred to simply as the Old Man—is the customary head of the Wai Daba house. I first met him when I travelled to East Timor, just after independence, in the year 2000. Quin's younger sister, Mena, had been a good friend of Marcia's and mine in Darwin and, as she happened to be visiting Timor at the same time, we made a trip out from Dili to Baucau and Bercoli. (This was a year before I met Quin: he had called me up when he heard his sister's friend had moved to Melbourne.) Because of that first early meeting, the Old Man takes credit for our marriage and loves nothing more than telling people it was only because Quin married me that he has now returned from Australia to the village. Despite his advanced years, the Old Man retains his handsome features and sharp, sometimes cutting, wit. While never formally schooled, he is intensely intellectual and political. When he has the chance, he talks of the region's history and politics, often lamenting what his life could have been if the Portuguese were not so selective about who they allowed to have an education. He would have loved to become a national political leader and steer the direction of the new nation. Once, as we sat together chatting on the back porch, he said: 'If I had been educated, I would have married a *malae*.' While this statement was perhaps referring to the utility or power of *malae* (which, interestingly, can mean foreigners, outsiders or nature spirits), I was not exactly sure about its implications, but his wife did not seem perturbed.

The house of Wai Daba, to which Quin's paternal grandmother also belonged, is the custodial house for the valley's main spring of the same name. In the past, the rice fields in the entire valley belonged to Wai Daba. At times when the local population was low, the ancestors of the Wai Daba house made agreements with outside kingdoms to send labourers to the area to help farm or tend lands. Many of the fields in the valley are still farmed by the descendants of these 'newcomer' families, some of whom married into the house of Wai Daba. As a result, many more families are now considered members of the house. But marital relations and land allocations are always historically complex and sensitive issues that involve a range of context-specific rights and obligations. The extent of these 'newcomer' rights in the land and resources is a topic of ongoing social negotiation, and periodic dispute.

One night, when we were staying at the Old Man's house on the main road, we discussed local land politics over dinner with him and other family members. Once most families had lived down in the valley or up on the savannah, but, during the Indonesian occupation, people were forced to relocate along the roadside, and most people remain there. Due to these often-forced migrations, there is a further degree of contestation in the village between those who have more recently come to farm on the land of others and those who assert ancestral ownership or use rights to the same land. Senior men and women still know these local histories. As a result of these elders' social knowledge and cultural capital, it seemed that simmering tensions in the village were largely kept at bay. But both elders and the younger people worried that if a new generation of customary leaders does not emerge to learn and pay close attention to these histories, unentitled others may usurp the land when the elders are gone.

At some point in our conversation, the Old Man asked me to help him find 'the book'. The location of this elusive book had been a frequent topic of discussion and it was not the first time he had brought it up with me. Indeed, it is a frequent topic of conversation and its loss an ongoing lament for the Old Man, as he explained to me years ago:

> What is important here is water. Our forebears were able to produce fields, rice and plantations because of this water. Our rice fields are old. In monarchical times before the Portuguese arrived, we already had them. We had no buffalo or horses; we would prepare the fields by dragging rocks through them. We would make a place and tie a rope to a piece of limestone and drag it around to make the soil muddy. There were no animals. And there was only a small amount of rice fields. These original rice fields were all named.

When the Portuguese arrived in the early twentieth century these fields were recorded in a book of tax records, but when our sacred house was burnt down [in the Indonesian era] that book was lost. In the past, my aunt, and Quin's grandmother, married a Chinese merchant in Baucau. She would pay the tax for this land. Her husband also worked with the Portuguese administrators and he would collect the tax for them.

The Portuguese sent only the children of the rulers they aligned themselves with to school—this was a kind of politics. If this hadn't been the case, we would all be smart by now. Bercoli is the heart of the Waima'a lands which stretched from here to the top of Matebian and across to Vemasse. While now these lands are largely dominated by the Makasae, it was the Portuguese that carved up the land.

In the Old Man's account, ancestral connections to the land and its waters are paramount, but it is also apparent that for him colonial-era taxation records are just as legitimate a witness to this reality. According to the Old Man, the book of records is important proof of land ownership in the context of disputes over rights to particular rice fields. The book, together with oral histories, proves the Old Man's contention that the descendants of newcomer houses were invited into the area and given rights based on land use, not ownership.

So, again, the Old Man asked me about the book. Had I been to Portugal to look for it yet? Had I made enquiries? I confessed sheepishly that I haven't yet had the opportunity; I don't speak Portuguese, so I needed to find someone who could help with the task. He was clearly disappointed. He wondered whether it might be in Macau. I could look there. He had heard from the Bishop of Baucau that many records from Baucau were kept in the Portuguese government archives in Macau. I solemnly promised that I hoped one day to be able to go to both places and investigate for him.

The following day, the Old Man's sister, Tia Martina, was to hold the ceremony to prepare her rice for carrying home. The day began with a ceremonial sacrifice of a chicken at the vent-like crevice hidden in the forest beside the Kai Bo'o fields. The chicken and the rice were cooked inside bamboo and some of it carried down deep into the crevice where if it was offered to the cave custodian with ancestral prayers. The rest of the chicken was taken to the *ulu* of the rice fields where the threshed rice lay in a huge pile on a side hillock. The chicken was arranged on a makeshift altar and laid out with baskets of rice containing eggs, betel leaves and areca palm nut. Here, more prayers were incanted. A goat had been killed but this was not part of the ceremony—'it's just for eating', said one of the uncles. This goat was a Timorese goat (*bibi Timor*), whereas in these fields only foreign goats (*bibi malae*) could be used for ceremony.

Later in the afternoon it was time for the threshed rice to be moved from the hillock into large storage bags. We were instructed by an uncle not to leave the ceremony area until it was finished and we had all eaten together. This is *lulik* or ancestral law. The uncle also told us that women may not enter the men's-only area while the rice-bagging ceremony was being carried out. Madalena and I passed the time with the other women and girls in a makeshift kitchen area. Tia Martina stood by the altar replete with offerings, periodically reaching into the baskets and taking out small handfuls of rice, which she sprinkled on the ground to feed the custodians of the area. She continued the feeding until the rice-bagging ceremony was over.

Quin filmed the ceremony up on the hillock and shared it with me. There was no prohibition on women viewing the ceremony, but, according to the culture of Wai Daba, they could not be physically present in the space. The ceremony began with an uncle, Tiu Vicente, placing several large baskets on top of the pile of threshed rice at the same time as thrusting a machete into its middle. The machete symbolises security, and the baskets delineated the area around which that security is extended. Through this ceremony, Tia Martina and her brothers who assist her were seeking the security of a prosperous rice-growing season the following year—their collective acts implored the ancestors to ensure that pests, extreme weather events or malign people do not attack the rice. Tiu Vicente prayed to the ancestors and began to fill the baskets with rice. The younger men then helped carry it over to the larger rice bag. Everyone was very keen to count how much rice had been harvested. In all, 59 baskets had been amassed, a number more than the previous year. The two large storage bags of rice, each holding approximately 30 baskets, hold a potential market value of around US$4,000.

Photo 38: Tia Martina carries out her part of the rice harvest offering.

Upon completion of the rice-bagging ceremony, the space was again opened up again for all to enter. The kids charged with glee up the hillock, beneath which huge piles of threshed rice stalks lay. They were free to roll, trample and bounce in the piles of hay to their hearts' content. Madalena and Zeca could not believe their luck; it was their first such experience of an event that would become a highlight over the coming weeks of the harvest. Rice stalk piles became some sort of surreal pop-up play centre. As the sun set, we looked up and noticed the forest's bat colonies on the move overhead. Bats, too, are ancestors.

Once the play was over, we were all called back to the cooking space. It was time to eat together. Everyone shared in the chicken, the goat, rice and eggs. Finally, we were each given a piece of betel leaf and nut as a blessing. It was late and very dark when we packed the kids in the car to return home. Our offer of a lift was declined by the Old Man. He walked home through the forest and rice fields alone—no doubt, checking the land for all sorts of propitious signs.

With each day in the fields I came to understand more about the significance and extent of these harvest ceremonies. At the same time, I had to accept that many aspects of this ritual world were out of bounds for me, now that I was actively participating in the family harvest. Back in 2013, the Old Man had allowed me to participate in and film the final new rice ceremony at the Wai Daba spring. Back then, my status as an academic (or journalist, as the Old Man prefers to call me) seemingly overrode the prohibition on women. But this time, he had stated, without further explanation, that I could not participate. There was an irony here: now I was an insider, I must play by the rules. In this case, the rules dictated that I sit on the outer. While the view from the inside is infinitely richer, it does not come without consequences for one's individual freedom.

***

Day by day, we came to appreciate the intricacies and seriousness of observing the customs of this world. One morning over breakfast, we learned more about the various harvest prohibitions such as a ban on taking peanuts and certain other foods into the fields. Once the Old Man told us about this, we quickly stopped the kids snacking on our stores of local peanuts (at least in the fields), but we had no idea of the reasons for this rule. 'Well,' said a cousin who had dropped in to visit, 'we must be very careful what we do in the valley'. He went on to casually describe the custodian of the rice fields as a very aggressive seven-headed snake. Even the removal of large rocks from the fields would cause him to retaliate. If he did, the Old Man, as the living human custodian of the site, would become sick straightaway. Newcomers to the valley must be especially careful of these custodians who are quick to attack. The kids' eyes widened. 'It's okay,' Noyti reassured us, 'the land knows who you all are.'

When we were harvesting rice near another spring, Wai Te, Quin and Zeca tried to sneak off to explore the area. They were warned to be very cautious. In hushed tones, we were told that, sometime ago, a being had emerged from the spring appearing to people in different forms. Sometimes it was a snake; another time it was a boat whose emergence created so much wind that the nearby candlenut trees toppled over. An unidentified white car (the kind driven by powerful people: foreign NGO workers, government people or clergy) had also been seen parked in the area. Wai Te was rumoured to host an entire city beneath its waters.

Each day as we laboured under the hot sun in the fields, we passed the time by gossiping about local life and happenings. Madalena and Zeca would help for a while, somehow avoiding slicing their fingers and feet with the deadly sharp rice sickles. After a while, they would wander off with their younger cousins to play or pick forest fruits. When Noyti and Luciana's older kids finished school each day around midday, they would join us and help in the fields, as would the children of whoever else was in the fields. Some children were more helpful than others, but, as a rule, the whole family helped out at harvest time. Some would occasionally climb the coconut palms fringing the fields, throwing down young coconuts that we would cut open and drink thirstily.

Photo 39: Lunch in Noyti's rice fields.

When it was just the women and me in the fields, the conversation would be in Waima'a, which I couldn't understand. But, if Quin was there, or if I was a part of the conversation, they would switch to Tetum. One day, the women got onto the topic of childbirth. Tia Martina had eight grown-up children. All except for her first child she had birthed at home alone. She said she preferred it that way. The women I was working alongside that day started talking about how absurd it was that doctors in Timor now advise women to stop physical work in the month or so prior to giving birth. They had all worked in the fields right up until the birth of each of their children. They said that work makes both mother and baby stronger, and that without physical labour women's bodies weaken and the babies are not moved along. They reasoned that this was why young Timorese women are increasingly experiencing complications in pregnancy and a higher frequency of caesarean deliveries. 'You've got to be careful of going to the hospital,' they said. 'Babies can die there.'

Another frequent topic of discussion was marriage and divorce. We talked about who was betrothed to whom and what was being exchanged in the process. We would spend hours talking about the various divorce proceedings underway and the attempts of families to reconcile outside of the court. The women worried that the new civil laws concerning marriage had done women a disservice, leading men to think it was their right to walk out and leave the women to look after the kids.

Medicinal plants were another frequent topic, often at my instigation. Sometimes we would come across a small plant or tree by the side of the fields as we cut the rice or took a rest. If I asked what it was, invariably the plant would turn out to have a medicinal use. Its leaves or bark or sap would be useful for certain known remedies. But the knowledge was clearly specialised and person-specific. One day I asked Noyti about a particular weedy grass common in the area we were working. 'What's this?' I asked. 'Oh, that's just grass,' she said. 'At least for me. For someone else it might have a use.'

Slowly I came to learn about women's deep knowledge of plants and their uses, how to collect them and how to prepare them. It always included a vast, but very personal, array of food and medicinal plants. Frequently, on our walks to the fields, the women would pick a particular plant to take home and prepare to treat one of their children or another family member. I recalled that a year or two earlier, when I had just begun researching health and healing and had asked these same women if they had medicinal expertise they would like to share, they would always decline or downplay their knowledge. I was usually sent off to interview men. I was coming to realise that this was knowledge and practice you had to learn by doing. Indeed, our own children's ailments, various rashes, cuts, scratches and bumps were typically the starting point for an intervention and visit to the forest pharmacopeia. Even our young nieces knew where to source the plants and how to prepare them to treat everyday ailments. Very often, these children were our doctors.

I noticed, too, how the women were in constant communication with the spiritual realm—even though they might deny it publicly. While formal ceremonies are usually men's business, talking with the ancestors or looking for ancestral signs is just as much women's as men's business. One day, as we chatted away in the fields and rain clouds began to loom on the horizon, one of the older women immediately cupped her hand to her mouth and blew in the air loudly. She looked at me with a smile. 'I am just letting the ancestors know to stay away—not to come yet—we are still harvesting the rice.' It seemed to work. The clouds soon cleared.

When we had finished cutting each area, we would switch gears for the next phase of the harvest. The younger men of the households would then start their labour. Their work involved collecting the harvested bushels of rice, tying them together and heaving them up to the area where the rice would be threshed using the valley's portable machine thresher. Almost gone are the days when the threshing was done by human foot or horse's hooves. What the machine can do in one day would have taken at least a week of work in the past.

In this phase of the harvest, it is the women's task to cook for the men, on site in the rice house or at home in the kitchen. They carried the prepared foods and hot coffee in large thermoses down to the fields on their heads (or, in my case, more awkwardly tucked under my arm). At this stage, women do much less of the hard, physical labour, although the cooking is still laborious and there is always the washing and looking after kids. Once the food had been prepared and delivered, the women would sit and chat in the rice house, catch up on happenings and gossip in a leisurely style. I enjoyed the chance to relax and listen, although I didn't understand much of what was said, let alone the hilarious jokes that would have them in stitches.

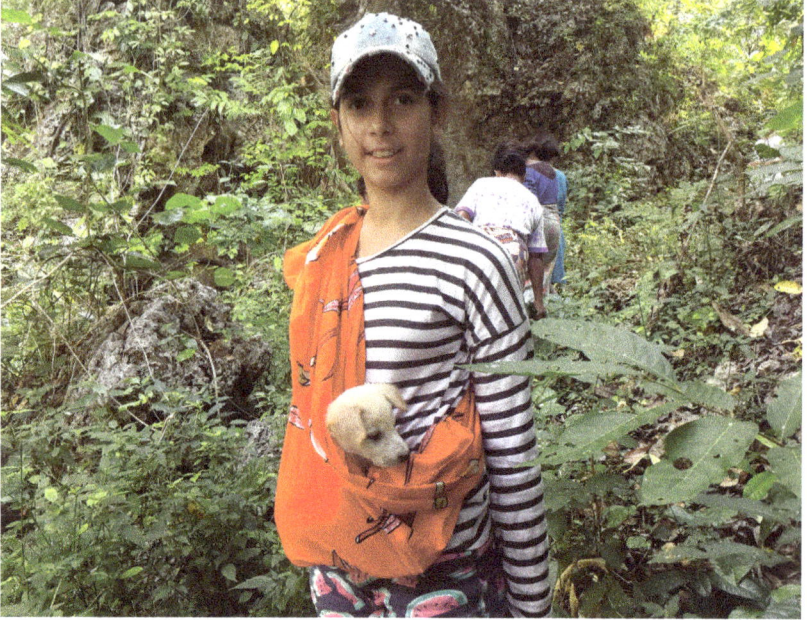

Photo 40: Madalena and Golden.

It was on one of these days that Zeca and Madalena received an unexpected gift. Sitting with the women under the afternoon shade of the rice house, one of the local teachers arrived holding a tiny white puppy under his arm. 'This is for them,' he said, pointing to the children. The puppy's mother, a scrawny white dog that belonged to the teacher, was milling about the fields where the rest of the teacher's family was also working. The mother dog had long since given up on the puppy. Apparently, one day when it had been out roaming the fields with its mother and siblings, it had fallen in a deep, dry, irrigation ditch and had not been able to get out. Some villagers living nearby had rescued it and taken care of it for several weeks. Now the teacher had reclaimed it for Zeca and Madalena. They had never had a puppy of their own and their eyes widened in disbelief and excitement. Later, when we were walking home, we fashioned a sarong like a baby sling around Madalena's shoulder. She carried the puppy in the sling back through the fields, proudly announcing to everyone that its name was Golden, after the colour of its ears. I sensed that the teacher and his family (descendants of 'newcomers' to the valley) were also quietly very pleased with this outcome. Golden was a gift who wove our family increasingly closer to the valley, perhaps subtly making us a little beholden to them.

While we were busy with the puppy, the men worked intensely, deftly operating the thresher to complete the task. Observing them, I was impressed by the highly choreographed ways in which each man or young boy would work and cooperate as part of a team. There was still a lot of manual assistance work to be done despite the use of the mechanised thresher. They appeared to effortlessly share and change tasks as needed, with some dropping out or slowing pace now and then, later coming back into the flow of work. The atmosphere was lighthearted. People seemed ever ready to share a joke, although, at certain points, when banter turned to national politics, merciless teasing between political rivals could create flashpoints of anger.

During this 2018 harvest, many of the younger men complained that they were too tired to work. None of them had slept much over the last month, instead gathering together each night to watch the football World Cup broadcast from Russia. The matriarch of the valley, Quin's elderly aunt Tia Brigita (or the Old Lady, as we called her), had no sympathy. She told them that in the past when people threshed rice by foot, people would be similarly deprived of sleep! Evenings would be full of dance, song, storytelling and collective trampling. Now satellite television was the culprit. Either way, there was work to be done!

Despite the goodwill, there was growing unease among the harvesters over what was to be done with this year's bumper harvest. Political unrest in the capital meant that for two rice-growing seasons in a row the government had not come as promised to purchase rice from the newly built rice stores in the valley. Despite a program known as '*povu kuda, governu sosa*' ('the people grow crops, the government buys'), government purchasers had not materialised. The people had duly changed their rice-production practices by switching to the higher yielding varieties, but now they could not sell their surplus. Similar situations across the country led to the coining of another more popular slogan, '*povu kuda, governu sae*' ('the people are the horses, the government ride them'). (*Kuda* can translate either as 'to grow crops' or as 'horse'.)

Just as economically profitable as rice crops, but more secure, was the sale of pigs. As soon as they were old enough, each of Noyti's five daughters had taken on the daily chores of helping their grandmother raise pigs in wood-and-thatch sties built at a distance behind the house. Raising pigs is laborious: the children's daily tasks involved the collection and cooking of substantial foodstuffs including husked rice bran, yams, coconut meat and household scraps. After working in the rice fields each afternoon, these children would also spend time with their mother and grandmother picking up old coconuts from the ground in the coconut groves, cleaving them open with a machete and digging out their hard flesh with knives. After also collecting bundles of firewood for cooking, they would bag the coconut meat and carry it with the wood on their heads back home.

When a pig reaches maturity, usually after seven or so years, it will be sold. The need for pigs in marriage exchange rituals means there are always plenty of buyers. The money raised from each sale, up to approximately US$800, is 'banked' for their children's future education. One day when we arrived home from the fields, we found one of Noyti's teenage daughters, Asandi, near the empty sty choking back tears. The pig had just been sold and its departure had affected her deeply. Through seven years of daily care, she had developed a great affection for the animal. She also knew, however, that its sale was her chance for a future education.

Photo 41: The purchased pig.

***

Towards the end of our time in the village, we killed a goat to celebrate Quin's birthday and invited our extended family from Bercoli and Baucau to attend a party. When Quin went with the Old Man to source the goat from the plateau above the village, the goat farmer resolutely refused Quin's payment. He remembered Quin's father having helped him during the resistance times and he wanted to honour that debt. At the same time as honouring a debt, the gesture created a new relationship. We were now obligated to the farmer, and it was understood that there would be plenty of time for us to reciprocate.

The goat meat and rice were cooked on an outdoor fire in bamboo lengths. Quin's older brother, Domingos, came from Baucau town to marinate the meat. Like Quin's father, and all his sons, Domingos is a renowned cook. My cooking skills over the open fire were well known to be much more limited and I was not usually asked to do tasks beyond collecting water, cleaning and peeling vegetables and washing up. Even the way I collected firewood lacked the required skills of discernment. But on this occasion, I was called to the kitchen to procure a can of our emergency stores of tuna and open it for Luciana's husband, the man who had slaughtered and prepared the cuts of goat. Despite his hours of work, he was prohibited by custom from eating meat. I was pleased that, with this simple act, I could autonomously feed someone.

After a lengthy process of food preparation and cooking, the meal was finally ready. The cooked meat and rice were first taken into the house and placed on an offering table in the main room, to feed the ancestral spirits. All the guests knew that the ancestors would be angered if they did not receive their share. Madalena and her cousins were sent off around the neighbourhood to collect bougainvillea and other flowers to prepare garlands that would later be cast over the ancestral graves. At the end of the day, a small party of us took these flowers and boxes of candles to the graveyard a little way down the valley. Noyti and another cousin came with us because they knew to whom each grave belonged. This was the first time that Quin had been to this graveyard: in the past, when the children were younger, we had always stayed in town during our visits and we would visit the larger graveyard where Quin's parents are buried. I asked if we were going to these Bercoli graves as a matter of course for a birthday celebration or especially because Quin was newly 'returned' to the village. I was told that you would never have a celebration like this in the village without involving the ancestors—they would be insulted. The visit to the grave was a way of saying 'we are still together with you'.

Life in these places is hard work. Returning home at the end of a long day in the fields, we would still need to pick fruit and vegetables from the gardens and forests along the way before preparing them and cooking for the large household, often without running water or electricity. While the electrical grid has now reached across the entire country, it is frequently unreliable. It almost felt as though the promise of electricity made it worse. Local households were now geared to a life dependent on power for pumping water and switching on lights. As a result, we were often caught off guard at night by last-minute power outages, left to function without the backup of kerosene lamps, rice cookers or stored drums of water. Still, we all preferred food cooked over the open fire. Despite the extra work it took to prepare, it was so much more flavoursome. We were especially pleased on these evenings when the Old Lady would make her signature dish, a kind of stir-fry of water taro stems freshly picked from the Wai Daba spring. This dish, which only she could cook successfully in our household, requires the utmost skill in execution. One wrong move, such as the use of metal utensils, and the delicious meaty stems would leave the insides of our mouths and throats itchy for hours. In contrast, the Old Lady's hands, they all said, were sweet (*liman midar*). Try as he might, Quin couldn't replicate her method.

We had come to the village hoping to give the kids an experience of rural life. We left immersed in another Timorese world. If only briefly, we lived a life wherein the hold of *lulik*—of the ancestors—is unquestioned. Their presence permeates the mind, the body, everyday relationships, practices and interactions. During our time in Bercoli, we were also made aware of the many current and potential disputes over rights to land and resources. Big questions loom over future pathways of inheritance and land use. But what had become clear was the depth of common concern to honour and respect their ancestors. And what flows from this respect, in both directions between the living and the dead, is the strength of families and communities practised in the arts of living together, not apart.

10

'The Geographical Tour'

With the rice harvest over, it was time for me to travel back to Dili to join Russell, my university colleague, and 20 of our geography students on a two-week study tour around Timor-Leste. During this field class, which I coordinate annually, staff and students are hosted in local communities and accompanied around the country by Timorese NGO the Haburas Foundation and a number of Timorese university students. The Haburas Foundation is East Timor's longest running environmental organisation, committed to enabling social justice and cultural preservation. It was founded by a group of RENETIL student resistance activists in the late 1990s and its inaugural and longstanding former director is Demetrio de Carvalho do Amaral. I have worked in a research capacity with Haburas for more than a decade, and Demetrio and his late wife Santi are Zeca's godparents.

We began planning for this field class in 2012, many years before it materialised. The communities we visit have long-term relationships with Haburas, which has helped local people establish the community-based tourism operations in the places we stay. Haburas staff are also long-time civil society actors and researchers into Timor-Leste's developing land laws, advocating consistently for the fulsome recognition of customary land and resource governance. As well as providing much-needed support to a range of community tourism initiatives across the country, our field class is a contribution to this activism at a number of levels. In 2018, Demetrio became the country's secretary of state for the environment, a position that allows him to exercise greater influence over environmental policies and practices in the new nation. While this has meant he no longer joins the field class, since our first 'tour' in 2016 he has continued to post on his social media pages about the field class and its engagement with rural communities. Our Haburas colleagues have dubbed the field class 'the geographical tour' and relish the opportunity to fashion it as something distinct from the usual development-focused study tours that percolate the tiny nation.

The field class is not easy to coordinate and it takes commitment and determined effort by all of us to maintain, honour and grow these relationships. Of course, Haburas do not invite us to share in this journey lightly; each event they enable and invite us to participate in is carefully chosen. Likewise, the Timorese communities we visit along the way have already carefully considered what they will share with our group and what should remain hidden from view; what will be included in, and what should be excluded from, our discussions.

Sometimes, during such encounters, the circumstances change and our hosts might decide to go further with what they want to share so that insider views and practices cross over into the public space. Usually this depends on the mood engendered, the energies generated by the group encounter and people's level of comfort with how the moment unfolds. For example, during the 2017 field class, one encounter at an origin house complex in the mountainous heart of the country involved the impromptu ritual sacrifice of a chicken and an augury, or reading of its entrails—an event that was both unexpected and deeply shocking for the students, a number of whom were vegan. Yet, for our host community, absorbed in the emotion of this particular event and intent on honouring Haburas and their special guests, this ritual symbolised the greatest honour they could bestow on our group, a sacrificial and celebratory act that would ensure the ongoing wellbeing and life flourishing of all concerned.

All of us involved in the organisation of the tour take a calculated risk in opening up ourselves, and our relationships of mutual trust, to ever-inquisitive newcomers: students from the University of Melbourne and Timor's national university. These newcomers are invited to learn from, witness, celebrate, record and contribute to the tour, and to relish in the intercultural encounters that work and to think together with us through those things that don't work and from which we can perhaps all learn more.

The tour works at many levels, taking up paths across the country, across histories, across cultures and across ourselves. The sharing of stories, the rhythms of various lifestyles and styles of communication, the grasping for relationships, the difficulties in the moments of miscommunication and in the cross-cultural confusion of some of these encounters are, for me, both the greatest joys and challenges of these two weeks. Such learning is never straightforward and there are many competing understandings and multiple expectations of what is happening, what is desirable and what is being desired in any given moment or encounter. Each year, a number of Timorese university students also join us on the tour and, without exception, they are excited for the opportunity to exchange ideas and learn with their Australian counterparts. Very often these students are learning about their own country at the same time. While all are familiar with and immersed in Timorese customary worlds, the fact that the tour prioritises and seeks out rural Timorese philosophies and practices comes as something of a revelation to many of them. On one occasion, early on in our time in the far east of the country, a young male Timorese student sought me out to express his concern that the Australian students were learning too much myth and not enough science.

***

During the third of these study tours that took place in 2018, our lead counterpart from the Haburas Foundation was Pedrito Vieira, a lean, tall man descended from Fataluku-speaking royalty. Pedrito was a former FALINTIL guerrilla and student resistance activist, and the son of the former (pro-integrationist) district administrator of Lautem. When he was jailed in Jakarta for his resistance activities, his father visited him there. Despite their political differences, the old man tearfully expressed his pride in his son for having such conviction to fight for what he believed in. Pedrito's late grandfather was a powerful man in the customary context, considered by many to be the king for the entire Lautem region.

After two days in Dili being briefed at Haburas headquarters, visiting the National Resistance Museum and the new National Centre for Memory, we set off for Pedrito's homeland. Leaving Dili we followed the entire north-eastern coast until we reached the tiny fishing village of Com. Pedrito's pick-up truck led our six-vehicle convoy all the way. Once we had passed through the border dividing Baucau and Lautem,

I felt Pedrito's disposition change and something else manifest. I could even detect a more assured driving style in the lead vehicle now we were in Pedrito's territory.

Com is situated on the edge of the country's first national park, a park named after the Fataluku-speaking FALINTIL resistance leader Nino Konis Santana. The heavily forested region and its mountainous caves had protected Santana and his men while they fought a guerrilla war against the Indonesian army for two and half decades. On our first night in Com we were welcomed into the village with a dance show performed by dozens of girls and a few boys. On this occasion, the girls were particularly impressive as they alternated between groups dressed in *tais* that performed traditional Fataluku dance, and short skirts and neckties reminiscent of American cheerleading. It seemed like the whole village had also come out to watch.

Earlier in the evening, Pedrito had introduced us to this place and explained how it had become a village during the Indonesian occupation. The entire population of the more mountainous inland region had been forced to move down to the coast. They were compelled by circumstance to give up their lives as farmers and learn to become fishermen. The population settled in a cleared section of a narrow coastal roadside where their life was highly controlled. Food was limited and the threat of violence ever present under severe repression by the Indonesians, who were trying to flush out the sympathisers of the FALINTIL. People could not travel far without raising suspicion, so agricultural activities were now very limited. In the beginning, they only had seed from the coastal tamarind trees to eat. That's why they began fishing.

Pedrito's voice broke as he explained this history to the group. I didn't need to look up; I could already feel what was happening. Each year on the tour we will experience moments like this, moments where it is suddenly no longer possible to keep a collective lid on the emotional well of the past. Somehow he managed to recompose himself and continue. As usual in these moments, it was hard for me to keep translating; I needed to stare at the ground to keep my emotions in check. Pedrito told us that during this early period the troops would go from house to house searching for FALINTIL supporters. Sometimes families would be forced to offer someone up just to placate the Indonesian forces. The story of Com is also Pedrito's story. The pain in his voice was almost unbearable. But his will to tell the story, to have us witness and honour the dead, was even stronger.

I found out later from another local man that his village was also in the hills above Com. He said that in the early 1980s his entire village was razed to the ground and all their animals were killed. The Indonesian military had been responsible for the incursion, I presumed. 'No,' he corrected me. 'By the FALINTIL forces.' He didn't elaborate other than to add that as a young boy it was very traumatic to see all their animals being killed and that the family had moved to another village. I was left reeling. When I asked Pedrito about such acts of violence by FALINTIL, he said it was likely carried out in retaliation towards the Indonesian military who were stationed in the village, not necessarily against the villagers themselves. Nonetheless, I cannot share these discussions with the students. I would not know where to start.

The next day, we visited a place dubbed 'Xanana's house' by everyone in Com, including the young kids (though I expect this is a fiction). What we saw was an 'eco-lodge' with various brick structures and a plunge pool languishing half built at the end of the new road leading from Com into the heart of the national park. People told us that a worker fell off the roof during construction a year ago, and that he was either still in hospital or dead. It seemed from various reports that the project had been abandoned for the time being. '*La halo on* [they have stopped it now]', said the kids on the beach. The owners of our guesthouse were more positive, suggesting that construction would soon commence. It was the guesthouse owners' clan who had authorised the building on the site and they were hoping that they would be offered the contract to manage the lodge.

Xanana's house has a bigger story. As my colleague Andrew McWilliam has written elsewhere, a new road to the government-funded eco-lodge has opened the gates for a local return to gardening and house building inside the national park. As our group walked along the newly graded road to Xanana's house, we noticed many new houses and elaborate vegetable gardens in construction. In other places, we saw what looked like new or refurbished stone and carved wooden objects, similar to those marking ancestral ceremony sites across the Fataluku landscape. To my surprise, there were even what looked like picnic spots with new seating fashioned out of wood. We stopped by one of these areas at a beautiful, long, white sand beach renowned for turtle nesting.

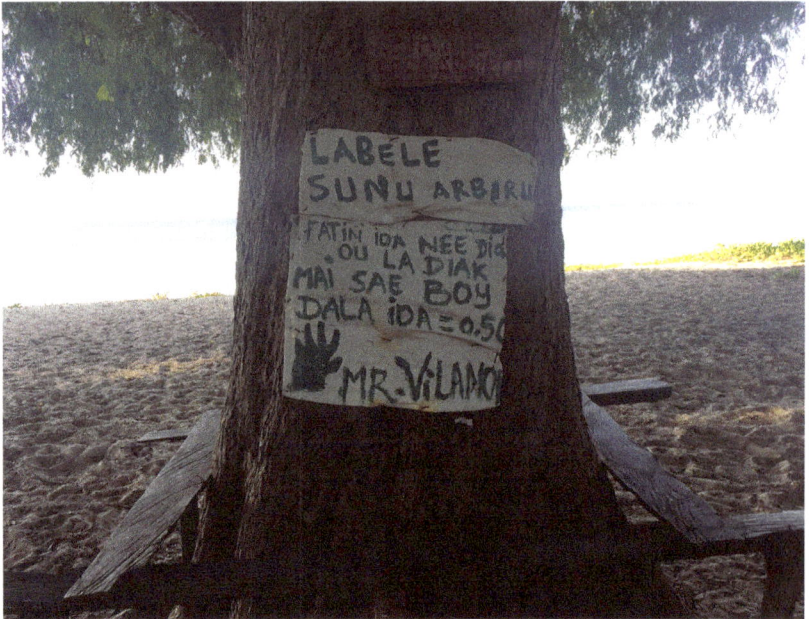

Photo 42: The 50-cent swing beach.

For reasons that became apparent, the children in Com know this area as *boy fatin* (the swing place). When we arrived, we were approached by an elderly man who lived in a newly constructed house nearby. He had created this picnic spot, as well as an elaborate swing made from fishing nets that was hanging from a branch. While we ventured out on the squeaky white sands to dip our feet in the turquoise sea and enjoy a quick rest (it was still a way to Xanana's house), the old man walked over and sat by the swing. He then told Atoo, one of the staff from Haburas, that our group would need to pay him 50 cents each for swimming at the beach. Atoo was surprised by a request for private payment in a national park and politely enquired as to the basis for the charge, at which point the old man indicated a handpainted sign in Tetum that was nailed to the tree by the swing. It had clearly been written by someone else, perhaps a park ranger, trying to placate the old man's pecuniary interests. Atoo didn't have the heart to tell him the actual wording of the sign: 'Whoever wants to play on this swing must pay fifty cents a turn.' While the children in Com may have coveted the swing, it was the beach that attracted foreign tourists and the beach for which the old man was seeking access payments.

Later that afternoon we visited an origin house belonging to Konu Ratu, the landowning clan of Com. We were accompanied by Pedrito and Senhor Fransisco, a senior clan member. The elaborately stylised and decorated wooden house, elongated on stilts with black palm–fibre thatching in classical Fataluku style, was situated by the beach road at the entrance to the village. It had been reconstructed in 2006 with funding from Portuguese donors whose name was now engraved on its front panelling. 'Fataluku origin houses are very expensive to build,' Senhor Fransisco told us. In the past, only certain clans could afford them. One of wealthier clans was the royal house of the region, Pedrito's own Chailoro. It was they, said Senhor Fransisco, who were responsible for supporting the Konu Ratu to build their houses both materially through marriage exchange between the houses and spiritually through ritual advice on the house-building process. The rebuilding of the Chailoro Ratu house would be an even larger undertaking.

Senhor Fransisco pointed out the Konu Ratu's original village site, which was in a coconut grove on an elevated ridge some distance from the coast. Konu Ratu sacred houses had been located there in the past. Nonetheless, he was quick to assert that Konu Ratu have always owned this land by the coast even if they had not always occupied it. Given our proximity to the sea, the students asked him if he was worried about the impact of sea level rise on the origin house built in this location. 'No,' he replied. 'The sea knows its boundaries.' The confidence in this statement was due to the large trees by the beach on the other side of the road that marked an ancestral border. 'The sea respects this,' he said. The students were puzzled. I explained that in Timor, border agreements are frequently made not just between those living, but also between the living and the dead. The trees were the living embodiment of that agreement.

Later, one of the students wondered at Senhor Fransisco's claims. Were they a sign of human arrogance: an assertion of mastery over nature? Another student remarked that she didn't see it as hubris because Fransisco was referring to an ancestral agreement between people and spirits of the sea. Neither observation left us any closer to unpacking the ramifications of climate change and sea level rise in the region. Anthropogenic climate change would have to be a discussion for another day.

Com's tourism peak was during the time of the United Nations peacekeeping missions. Given that few tourists come to Com these days, as soon as our vehicles drove into the village, the local kids had made a beeline for the beachside edges of our guesthouse. Small groups of siblings of all ages intently worked the zone, imploring the students to make a purchase. It was hard for the students to resist the onslaught and most bought something. Before we left Com, Pedrito made an announcement requesting the students to surrender the handmade shell necklaces they had bought from local children on the beach. 'Don't worry,' said Pedrito, 'you will get them back when we return to Baucau.' The students looked perplexed, perhaps sheepishly wondering if they shouldn't have been trading in local shell life after all. I don't think any of them expected what came next. Pedrito explained that we were about to leave Com and visit a large freshwater lake, Iralalaru, on the raised plateau in the middle of the national park. In the lake region, the Fataluku customarily do not allow the mixing of freshwater and saltwater substances. Were we to take these shells from the sea up into the lake area, we could bring calamity upon all. The request to hand them in was so they could be stored in a relative's house before we entered the lake region.

The Konis Santana National Park is an International Union for the Conservation of Nature (IUCN) community-protected area. At the lake, we met with one of the lake custodians, Senhor Hermingildo, and a park ranger. The old man arrived on the back of his son's motorbike; he wore farm clothes and gumboots almost as long as his legs and carried only a small pouch containing betel chew, some uncooked rice and an egg. The park ranger, who we had picked up on our way through the nearby village, was dressed in a badged uniform and carried a clipboard fastening several pages of typed text. The latter was a long list of the scientific names of endemic tree and animal species identified by foreign researchers working in the national park. Later, when answering the array of questions posed by the students about the national park, he would periodically scan this list for any useful information he could add. For the ranger, the list was a necessary public declaration of state authority over the area.

As in previous years, the lake custodian carried out a ceremony at the Irasiqiru river, a watercourse that runs out from the lake before disappearing down a sinkhole several kilometres downstream. The ceremony involved cracking an egg by the river and sprinkling some rice grains into the water. At the same time, the lake custodian blew onto the foreheads of Russell and me, as the group's representatives. He was letting the non-human custodians of the lake know that our group was visiting. He also checked with us as to whether any of our group from the previous year had gotten sick or had some disaster befall them. (In fact, one student had been hospitalised in Baucau following our last visit to the Irasiqiru. But we didn't mention this incident to the lake custodian because, after much discussion, the Haburas staff had attributed the student's illness to an attack by land spirits on the island of Jaco. While Russell and I were busy with the student in the hospital, they had been privately busy organising a spiritual intervention to counter the attack. The student remained unaware of the full treatment they had received to recover their health.)

Russell explained the geomorphology underpinning the formation of the lake's karst landscape and what is known about its complex hydrogeology from the perspective of Western science. Senhor Hermingildo, meanwhile, told the students the story of the lake's origins—of how a village lay in the centre of the once dry area until, one day, waters rose up out of the ground, swallowing the village and most of its people. Senhor Hermingildo said that sometimes the custodians beneath the lake still seek out the company of descendants from this village and, to do this, they must take a life from this world into theirs. He tells us that his own sister was harvesting watercress in the river one day when she was taken by one of the ancestral crocodiles.

Photo 43: Students at Iralalaru and the Irasiqiru river (Demetrio speaking with Senhor Hermingildo standing at rear).
Source: Russell Drysdale.

The students asked Senhor Hermingildo how he became a custodian of the lake. He explained that he had been chosen by the spirits of the lake:

> You will know when you have been chosen, but you may hide it from others. Others will notice, though, when you start to change and know things and do things you didn't before.

These spirit communications were first conveyed to him in dreams. The students wondered about who would take over from him. He disclosed that this worried him. People would continue to be chosen by the spirits, as he had been, but would the newer generations be receptive to their gift? Would they even be prepared to take on the responsibility? He was not sure. With his own two sons working overseas in England and Australia, he could not be certain about them taking on his role. The students were surprised that his family members were so far way. As far removed from their own reality as this place seemed, its people are, like them, deeply embedded in a globalised world. In recent years, Timor-Leste's largest non-oil export has been sending workers to the developed world. Tellingly, many of the two-storey concrete houses springing up around the edges of the lake were built from the remittances provided by family members who work overseas, mostly in meatworks and other factories in Ireland and England.

The previous year our conversation with Senhor Hermingildo had taken a very different turn. The pressing matter at that time was the infighting that had been observed between the crocodiles of the lake. One particularly vicious fight had ended in the death of a large male crocodile. Senhor Hermingildo's voice dropped as he pointed out an area further downstream away from the lake's edge and offered a revelation that upturned any idea we might have had that this was a 'natural' battle of territorial animals:

> Just over there is where they meet. The crocodile commanders of the lake. Each of them represents one of the seven clans with custodial responsibilities for the area. They meet here regularly to negotiate with each other.

People in the area understood that something had gone wrong to upset this normal course of negotiation. The alliance between the commanders had been broken and they had turned on each other. The root cause was thought to be disharmony in the community of the living. Tensions from this realm had spread into the ancestral realm. The death of a crocodile commander had given everyone living around lake pause for reflection and deep concern. Recounting the story in Fataluku and then retelling it to me in Tetum so I could translate it into English for the students also gave Senhor Hermingildo, Pedrito, the park ranger and other Haburas staff and locals time to ruminate on the issues under discussion. As I translated the long and culturally complex explanations of the lake area that were given to me, all of the others would be engaged together in very lively conversation in Fataluku. The students looked on, mystified.

The locals told us that they didn't know exactly why their ancestors were fighting; they were still trying to get to the bottom of the conflict. Senhor Hermingildo and others had been to the commanders' site to carry out a ceremony and ask for peace to be restored in the ancestral world. They mentioned one suspicion that the cause was due to breaches in cultural protocols relating to development in the area. They recounted how a local village chief, who had recently brought a truckload of sand from the sea to use in a large two-storey house construction around the lake, had later suffered the death of all his buffalo.

They told us, and we could see ourselves from their animated discussions, that they needed to assess very carefully these happenings in the 'natural' world and respond accordingly. Later on in the afternoon, two of these commanders came patrolling downriver. The intimidatingly larger of the two travelled past where our group was gathered some distance from the banks and turned 180 degrees in the water. There it lay for a long time, staring at us. No wonder Senhor Hermingildo was keen to know that we had all been okay on our return to Australia.

Crocodiles are always a frequent topic of conversation on the study tour. In order to properly nourish these human–animal relationships and to respect their boundaries, in some parts of Timor where crocodiles are prevalent, customary elders have communicative ritual responsibilities referred to as 'marrying crocodiles' (*kaben ho lafaek*). Very often, we hear, it is people who do not pay enough respect to either these cross-species connections or these boundaries who are the subject of attack. Crocodile attacks are increasing; statistically, people in Timor are now 10 times more likely to die from crocodile attack than from malaria (a disease that is trending in the opposite direction). DNA research by Australian scientists is investigating whether there are links between increased Timorese crocodile attacks and foreign crocodiles journeying across the Timor Sea from the overpopulated crocodile territories of northern

Australia. The Timorese are very interested in this research into 'wild' crocodiles and the implications it may have for the relationships between customary communities and their ancestral crocodiles. In the meantime, the government has placed bright yellow crocodile dangers signs at known crocodile sites around the country, including the place where we sat that day by the Irasiqiru.

After we heard from Senhor Hermingildo, the rangers spoke with us about their ongoing struggles to manage the conservation values of the national park. As an IUCN community-managed park, timber felling and hunting are not banned in their entirety, but management does seek to regulate these activities. There is much confusion about the rules and a fear of complete hunting bans. The park rangers explained that they are desperately under-resourced and must *lao ho liman mamuk* (walk country with empty hands). With little in the way of resources or enforcement powers, they must use their customary negotiation skills to work through customary elders like Senhor Hermingildo to address illegal activities. Their jobs as mediators between local people and the state, while critical and very difficult, were not properly recognised by either party. But, as one ranger said: 'I do it for my nation.'

The following day, another custodian of the national park area, Senhor Nus, took us to visit a cave where his ancestors had lived and where some were buried. Senhor Nus had resided in Indonesia for some time and had only relatively recently returned to the area. He was now determined to reassert his custodial responsibilities for the site and had immediately started working at the Valu Sere beach bungalows (tourist accommodation established in 2007 by a collective of the area's landowning clans). On the main road descending from the lake towards the cave and the coastal community tourism establishment, a new official sign read: 'Lene Ara Archaeological site 200 metres this way'. During our visit to the cave, I asked about this new sign. Senhor Nus confirmed that it had been put there by staff from the Ministry of Culture and expressed his concern. The custodians of the area had asked for government protection in addition to the traditional stone barrier outside the cave marking out the area as a *lulik* space. During the occupation, many such caves had been inhabited by FALINTIL hiding in the jungle. It was this *lulik*, manifest in different ways and sites across the whole area, that is credited for keeping the fighters alive. At the time, the resistance fighters did not need special permission to enter caves because the period was understood by the living and the ancestral realm alike as a 'state of emergency'. The land and spirits understood that people needed their protection without them having to first seek it. But things were different now. The ancestors were demanding their dues and, consequently, the people were reinstating their careful custodial responsibilities and communications with the ancestral realm. When we left the cave, the custodians lingered to say a small prayer before leaving some coins on the rock as an offering. What effect the new sign on the road and unchecked visitation would have on the relationships with the ancestors was, as yet, unknown.

While the Timorese university students who accompany us each year readily invoke their own ancestral relationships and responsibilities, as is the case for most Timorese engaged in formal education, they are also devout Christians. The Australian students are always surprised to learn that these ostensibly modern and highly fashion-conscious young students, who seem to share with them similar dreams and aspirations for the future, might also attend church services in Dili every day of the week. One morning over breakfast at Valu Sere, I was chatting with two of the female Timorese students, Mafi and Ti. They were looking to me for some clarity following a bewildering conversation with some of the Australian students with whom they were beginning to form close friendships. 'They don't believe in God!' said Mafi. 'One said they believe in "spirit" but which spirit? Who looks after them when they travel far? What is the purpose of their life?' Before I could answer, they told me that they had tried to reassure the students that God loves them in any case, even if they didn't believe. Ti told me how she had just been to Japan on a study tour. Although a fervent believer in God (for her, God comes first), she had rung her parents in her home village while she was in Japan and asked them to seek the protection of the ancestors of their origin house while she was away.

Obviously appreciating the chance to speak frankly on these matters, Mafi added that she would put her relationship with her ancestors before God, but she reiterated that both were important to her. What had really floored them was the Australian students' lack of relationship with the divine or the ancestral world. 'What do they believe in?' they asked me with concern. '*Sira fiar an*,' I offered weakly. 'They believe in themselves.' 'Oh my God,' said Ti, completely incredulous. 'It is unbelievable. I feel sorry for them.'

11

Carrying the Name Forward

As opportunities arise on the study tour, I make a point of discussing land issues with Timorese tertiary students. One day, a young Timorese woman explained to me that women from her rural area didn't have rights to land. This wasn't a problem, she said, if a woman married a man. However, her concern was about how to be independent as an unmarried woman. How could she acquire some land for herself? She surmised that her best option would be to buy land in Dili or in one of its rapidly growing peri-urban areas where modern land markets were emerging—but costs there were often prohibitive. Another female student said her priority was not her own access to land, but in making sure her parents were secure in their rights to their land in the mountains. 'As long as they are secure,' she said, 'I can feel secure—I will have the shade and protection of my house.' She contended that many of her peers in Dili (male and female) felt the same way. 'They are looking for knowledge and skills to take them forward in life, not land.'

During the same conversation, a young male student added that, while he had the right to land through his parents in a remote area, he, too, wanted to live in Dili. The problem is not only that land is so expensive in Dili, but also that land titles are insecure. He said that people know from bitter experience that the government will often use their executive power to acquire land, and that makes many people, no matter their gender, worry and feel insecure.

Rights to land, particularly women's rights to land, have been identified as a major issue in post-conflict Timor. New land laws had been rolled out over the previous years, and the aid and development sector had invested heavily in promoting women's rights to land and property. It was not just foreigners that were talking about these issues; increasingly, it was also a topic of discussion and a priority among young, educated Timorese women. The potential for the emerging 'women's movement' and associated gender laws and policies to intersect with the cultural context of Timor-Leste was now the subject of critical debate.

These types of discussions about gender and land rights are harder to have in a village setting. In my experience, rural women rarely reflect on the gender dynamics of their situation that are often asserted (by others) to be unequal. Nonetheless, by listening closely to the conversational preoccupations of rural women themselves I have been able to discern nuances in women's concerns around issues of status and power in their own lives.

Rural women frequently talk about their own role, alongside the men, in securing and carrying forward their rights and obligations for familial lands and property. This role is especially pronounced in discussions of past conflict and the hardship suffered under the Indonesian occupation. Women are especially proud that through dark times they kept their customary practices and relationships alive and strong wherever possible. With many men away fighting or working (for either side), it was women who tended to graves and other sites in the landscape, nourishing their family's relationships with the ancestors and others. The other side of this role is memory work—the tendency by women to catalogue, and frequently voice, past misdemeanours or discriminations suffered by a woman and her children (often at the hands of extended family members): who did what, at which event and when; who refused to participate; who withheld an exchange; who traded insulting words. This catalogue of personal slights and intimate complaints reveals both the strengths and the tensions around customary practices.

In all the stories I have heard, I rarely detect any lament about women's supposedly inferior role to men. Rather, these women's concerns follow different paths. A major preoccupation is the lack of respect now extended by the younger generations to their elders. Another is the discrimination towards people from the rural areas by those from the city. In terms of familial tension, marriage relations between houses and ongoing exchanges between the houses is often a cause of concern. This is especially the case when family members perceive a man as giving higher priority to his wife's family than to his own house, and vice versa. The particulars of what was or wasn't exchanged in marriage arrangements is a frequent topic of discussion. The ledger might include references to incidents that occurred decades ago at wedding parties and other life cycle events, which women are usually responsible for organising and resourcing. In the rural areas, all people—especially women—are keenly aware of issues and obligations around status and expectations of cultural protocols. Transgressions of any of these arrangements, particularly among women themselves, are keenly recorded and often referred to.

One day in Bercoli, we were chatting with one of Quin's aunties about recent happenings in the family. She told us that her husband had just left on a trip back to his home village in the mountains. He was involved in negotiating the marriage arrangements there for a nephew who was to marry a woman from a coastal hamlet closer to Baucau. It had turned out, however, to be a very complicated intergenerational negotiation. While the girl and her mother resided in the coastal hamlet, neither of the girl's parents originated from there. The girl's father, who was dead, was from a family in another area of the mountains. The girl's elderly mother was from a coastal village to the west. These facts were of great importance to the marriage negotiation, particularly as the mother's family had never received any marriage benefits from the father's family. To enable the marriage of their daughter, the debts of the father's house to the mother's house must first be paid.

In practice, this meant that the offering from the nephew's family to his bride's family—10 buffalo, 10 horses and US$3,000 in lieu of traditional swords—must take these intergenerational debts into account. While the gifts were ostensibly being made to the girl's father's house in the mountains, this house had to immediately regift them to the girl's mother's house on the coast further west. Without the settlement of these debts, the daughter's marriage could not proceed. The mother's house, too, had obligations in concluding this exchange. The requisite pig, female *tais* and male *tais* were duly taken and presented by the mother and her family to the deceased husband's house. In turn, the girl's mother had now become a full member of her husband's house, and, though she continued to choose to live elsewhere, upon death she would be buried in her husband's village. In turn, the deceased father's house gifted a pig and two *tais* to the nephew's house in the mountains. This obligation of gift giving, especially to a woman's origin house, would continue for these fertility takers at each significant life cycle event into the foreseeable future.

Such exchanges are never formulaic. After Tia Martina explained the intricacies of these transactions, another of Quin's aunties added that her own origin family is prohibited from exchanging pigs between intermarrying houses. Instead, they must gift to their in-laws rice, woven cloth and money. Pork may be offered in some exchanges, but the animal must be dead so as not to violate an ancestral sanction on the exchange of pigs. As is more common than generally acknowledged, Tia Martina had not married out of her origin house. In an arrangement that defied the 'ideal', which, in a patrilocal area, is for women to marry into their husband's houses, her husband, from the mountains, had married into her house. What is important to recognise is that, whichever 'pathway' is followed, the status of some of these marital exchanges often remains indeterminate and is the subject of negotiations over very long periods. This contingency keeps relations between houses alive. This is not a situation of fixed rules and processes as is so often imagined by outsiders.

***

According to Quin's cousin Noyti, when the daughters of a house marry outside it, some residual rights will usually remain. Her two married sisters, for example, continued to have use rights over rice fields in their home village and one sister had built a house on the family property. Noyti had been given land exclusive to her by her parents because her husband, from West Timor, had married into her house. In such cases, women are obliged to prioritise the needs of their birth family above those of their husband's family.

Noyti's brother had married a woman from Manatuto, an area of Timor where many houses transfer land matrilocally, but because he was the family's only son, his wife had married into the Bercoli customary system. Indeed, probably because they only had one son, the Old Man and his wife had largely avoided formal marriage exchanges with all their daughters' husband's families. They preferred to keep all their daughters, to some extent, inside the house. Rather than a dogmatic adherence to 'ideal' social arrangements, the reality of life in rural areas is much more fluid. What people prize are cultivated skills in the adaptive art of living together, and in negotiating often indeterminate status and power relations. It is, above all else, relationships that matter. Pathways can always be negotiated.

Over dinner one night with the Old Man, complex issues were raised concerning the impact of emerging state land laws and, in particular, women's rights to land. As was typical, he quickly began to express his frustration—anger, even—at a perceived failure by the Timorese state to properly think through the implications of importing foreign laws into Timor-Leste. He was particularly incensed by the new land laws that prioritised more recent occupation of land over people's ancestral rights and obligations to an area. In relation to women's rights to land, he was adamant that there were already pathways to women's rights and recognition under customary arrangements. At its most basic level, he told us, activating these rights depends on the politics of the existing land tenure system. How these rights emerge will depend on whether the local system is patrilocal, matrilocal or both (ambilineal). It also depends on histories and patterns of migration into the area. Due to population migration, any area might have several different systems.

In every case, there would be an identified head of the family and head of the household. In a patrilocal system, it will usually be the man who is the head of the family and the woman who is head of the household. In a matrilocal system, or in a situation when a man has married into a house in a patrilocal system, it is the opposite. The Old Man reminded us that his sister had inherited full rights to her land through her parents. In this case, this was because her husband, who had come from elsewhere during the Indonesian occupation, had no family to support him in his marriage negotiations. There was no one to speak for him and to provide the prestations necessary for marriage exchange. As a result, 'his name is now smaller than that of his wife'.

But the Old Man maintained that, even when prestations are exchanged, it is never the case that a woman has 'no name'. Indeed, following the exchange of such goods, a woman's name and her status will always be upheld, not only during the woman's lifetime, but also throughout the lives of her children and her grandchildren. Ritual gift giving ensures that the prestige attached to a woman's rights and recognition is maintained intergenerationally. Such rights and recognition are activated and reactivated through time. The Old Man explained that when people exchange ritual gifts through marriage, their own name and that of their house are also carried in the exchange:

> To have a name means we are someone, we have rights, we have connections and networks that need to be considered and honoured—through time. To have no name is something different. This is not to exist into the future.

From the Old Man's lengthy explanation, I understood that giving individuals equal rights to land in a Western legal sense acts to cancel out these spaces of recognition, connection and their intergenerational surety. New laws may create for people rights in the 'now', but, as land is bought and sold between individuals, these rights can be alienated. The practices that uphold intergenerational rights and obligations over the long term were becoming less important than the rights and interests of individuals now. For both men and women, profound shifts were underway in their customary ways of relating to land and each other.

***

Towards the end of our time in Bercoli, the Old Man's wife, Tia Brigita (the Old Lady), began speaking to me with an uncharacteristic frankness about the changes occurring in people's residential status and rights to land. Land must be shared more equally, she said. Women also have rights to land. But the localised processes surrounding new land laws meant that people were becoming fixed in their thinking about ownership and getting into terrible disputes over land and resource rights. They needed to work towards compromise, she said. They need to restore and work more than ever towards a better sharing of the land, especially within families.

The Old Lady is extremely hardworking and, in her own way, very kind. She is also intensely proud and readily offended. When she was at home and not in the fields, she was often visited by her younger sister, a widow who had recently lost her son and who now cared for her many grandchildren while their mother worked in the fields and travelled to sell produce in the Baucau market. During these animated chats they would sit by the kitchen chewing betel nut and gossip about any recent dramas in the family or the village. I would sometimes join them, although I always tried to be very careful about what I did and said around the Old Lady. I think we were both a little wary of each other, circling carefully around an incident that had happened many years before.

Photo 44: The Old Lady in her rice fields.

That was in 2013, when the entire family and extended networks were gathering together in the Baucau house preparing for my father-in-law's funeral. He had passed away in Australia, a place where he had been medically evacuated to following a motor vehicle accident and stroke two years earlier. People were descending in waves on the house to prepare for the arrival of his body and the ensuing funeral. Much of this activity involved animal slaughter and food preparation. There was unbridled sorrow that this great patriarch had died so far away from home and emotions were running high among the immediate family.

One day I had been absent from the kitchen for most of the morning. I had been trying to get a fast enough internet connection to transfer money back to Australia to assist with the cost of his coffin and repatriation. Quin, wanting a record of this mass gathering in his father's honour, asked me to go and film the activities underway. As I filmed, I heard the Old Lady's voice behind me. She was loudly bemoaning, to everyone gathered in the space, that none of the daughters-in-law from the Baucau house were doing any work. Her comments were a public shaming that tipped me, in that moment, past breaking point. I packed up my camera and tripod and headed back to our part of the house in tears. Someone told Quin, who, despite my protestations, went to speak with the Old Lady about what had just happened. She quickly arrived in the room and tried to assure me that her comments were directed at the other daughters-in-law, not me! Her outburst, Quin told me later, had been a very public way of ensuring that all the daughters-in-law, but some more than others, were brought into line. Nonetheless, after this incident, Acinling, one of Quin's sisters, decided it was better to keep me away from the kitchen all together for a while. I was given the job of sitting by the altar, keeping my father-in-law's spirit company while we waited for his body to arrive.

In 2018, the Old Lady's commentary was again connected to events in the town where family relationships had gone awry. We had received a call one morning from two of Quin's brothers in Baucau. They were desperate for the Old Man to travel down to the town and broker peace. A dispute between their wives had led to a violent altercation between a niece and her aunty. Outraged at the disrespect shown by the niece to their mother, two of her sons had gone on a violent rampage, damaging property and yelling out insults in full view of the town. To make matters worse, news of the dispute had spread like wildfire. Nieces and nephews from across Timor and overseas were engaged in name-calling and mudslinging through social media. While intra-family disputes were not uncommon, it was the public elements of this dispute, especially the online posts, that most alarmed the family. To be publicly disrespected and shamed is the ultimate insult in Timor. Emotions within the family were running high.

The Old Man reluctantly went to town, and Quin went along with him. There things went from bad to worse. Rather than being given the opportunity to broker peace, the Old Man found himself in the middle of a heated argument in which his grandchildren were threatening each other with physical violence. One of them was even holding a metal grinder he had picked up from a pile of construction materials on the veranda of the house. Another nephew who was a policeman arrived to restore order, and the Old Man quickly gave up trying to negotiate a solution and returned to Bercoli fuming with anger and disappointment. After we heard what had happened, all of us back at the house in Bercoli were outraged. That the family were disrespecting each other was bad enough, but worse was that they were also disrespecting the Old Man, who they had earlier called on so desperately for help.

No one said it publicly, but at its core the dispute was about property. The conflict arose over the rights of the various siblings and their families to live in and control various parts of the sprawling urban block.

The property containing completed and partial houses, and occupying a prime site in the middle of town, was the life's work of Quin's father. Now he was dead, there were deep animosities over sibling claims to inherit the property, all of which were contingent and complicated. Since their father had died, six of his grown-up children had occupied parts of the property, and most had children who were now coming of age. Yet these property tensions, which had no doubt fuelled the animosity between the wives, were not matters anyone wanted to discuss in the context of this dispute. Claims were a matter for the siblings to sort out, not their spouses. In the meantime, reconciliation was needed over the damaged property and ruptured relationships. Despite the first failed attempt at brokering the peace, the father of the niece who had insulted the aunt travelled to Bercoli and pleaded for the Old Man to return and help sort out the dispute. While he had no doubt been expecting the request and acceded to it, the Old Man made it clear he was returning to the town very reluctantly.

I had witnessed these situations before. I still carried the emotional scars from the intra-family altercations that had erupted during the time of my father in-law's illness and death five years earlier. I knew too well the kinds of hostility that would play out among this group of hot-headed siblings, and I didn't want to be a part of it. Besides, I reasoned, I didn't want Madalena and Zeca exposed to that kind of conflict. While Quin and the Old Man headed back to town, the Old Lady and I stayed in the village gossiping with the other family members and condemning the townspeople for their general lack of civility: 'And they say we are just mountain women in sarongs!' said the Old Lady. 'They have no respect,' we all agreed.

While I am used to family conflict, the potential for violence in these kinds of altercations frays my nerves. I worry that Quin will get embroiled, too, and that things will get further out of control. While everyday life in Timor is relatively safe, people fear the violence that springs forth in heated intra-family disputes, and while such conflict is not welcomed, it is also not shied away from. Conflict and its resolution are the reality of life in small societies where people must learn to live together through thick and thin.

When the Old Man and Quin returned to Bercoli, we were told a date for the formal reconciliation ceremony at the Baucau house had been agreed. I was expected to attend too, they both told me. Despite my foreign

ISLAND ENCOUNTERS

sensibilities (or weak constitution) in these matters, it was made clear that, as one of the family, I was expected to be a part of the reconciliation. In these situations, all family members have a role to play, even if it is only to witness the reconciliation. As further justification, they said: 'You study culture; here is another chance.'

A week or so later, most of the siblings had already pooled money for the purchase of the sacrificial buffalo for the peacemaking ceremony. At close to US$1,000, this purchase was not a trivial undertaking. But, in the final day or so leading up to the event, the brother married to the aggrieved aunt made it clear that they would not be contributing to the purchase. This signalled to all that they were not prepared to recognise their role in the collective wrongdoing. In fact, he said, his wife's rural family would not accept the terms. For them, it was their sister's honour that had been publicly affronted both in the town and online and it was she who must receive the apology. Her honour had been defamed to the 'whole world' when one of the niece's older siblings responded to the violence of the aunt's children by posting on social media that 'obviously' their rural cousins' families had no education or manners.

With the money for the buffalo purchase already collected and the date set by the Old Man, most of the rest of the family felt the need to proceed with some kind of reconciliation event. On the set date, we all gathered on the main veranda of the property and waited to be joined by the aunt and her family. She did not come, angrily telling her husband that this problem related to his family and he could sort it out. Someone called a priest who was well known to the family, and when he arrived word was sent of his arrival to the aunt. The priest was the godfather to one of her children and he made it clear to her, very diplomatically so as not to override the customary authority of the Old Man, that he had come to broker another kind of peace: peace through the forgiveness and grace of God.

After what felt like an interminable period of time, the aunt made her entry onto the veranda. The niece and her parents swooped in immediately to make their peace offering, with the niece prostrating herself in front of her aggrieved aunt, a woman who was half her size and three times her age. As she begged forgiveness, the niece's mother stood in solidarity behind her and then handed her sister-in-law an envelope containing US$200. The money was equivalent to that of a horse, which custom dictated was an essential exchange for the resolution of this kind of conflict. With the priest and the Old Man looking on, the aunt reluctantly received the peace offering. She then sent one of her disgruntled brothers, who had been seated at the edge of the veranda, up to her house to fetch a *lipa* (sarong). When he returned, she opened the tubular cloth and slipped it over her niece's head and body. They embraced and started to cry, and then the niece's mother joined the embrace, also suddenly weeping. All the other feuding cousins present also came humbly forward out of the shadows. Everyone began to embrace each other and cry.

The peacemaking had been cathartic for us all. I, too, was crying, as was Quin. The depth of feeling and history tied up in this moment was evident. I had seen these nieces and nephews grow up together over nearly two decades. To see them embroiled as young adults in their parents' long-simmering antagonisms was sobering for all concerned. On this day, a resolution of sorts had been reached, but the core issues were far from resolved. We sealed the reconciliation by sitting down to eat together, the Old Man and priest at the head of the main table surrounded on all sides by the gathered family members.

Despite the temporary reprieve in hostilities, the dispute lingered on. Neither aunt visited the other's part of the property and the truce between the cousins felt uneasy. The niece moved back to live and attend school in the capital where she and her siblings had been born. A buffalo was yet to be sacrificed to acknowledge collective wrongdoing. The Baucau property felt, as it had many times in the past, like a tinderbox.

But another event loomed. Twelve months or so later one of the niece's older brothers was to marry in a lavish wedding in the capital. The question was whether the feuding families would truly reconcile for this event? We breathed a sigh of relief when, back in Australia, we saw pictures on social media of the aggrieved aunt and her family attending the wedding. The significance of their participation could not be overstated. Despite the lingering tensions over property and family honour, the desire to conform to the greater good of fostering intergenerational wellbeing had again won out above all.

12

Opening the Paths
to Healing

During our final two months in Timor-Leste, I was immersed in documenting the practices and knowledge of specialist and everyday healers in Baucau and its hinterlands. In previous research trips, we had usually left the children at home with their cousins, but now they were older we encouraged them to come with us so they could experience a greater breadth of Timorese life. One of our first visits was to the house of Senhor Januario whose home is in a village on the plateau above Bercoli. Januario da Silva is a renowned local bone healer. Himself an avid cockfighter, he maintains that he learnt his craft by healing cockerel injured from fighting. In the Indonesian era, his first patient was an Indonesian soldier injured during a soccer match. But the military doctors had been angered by his intervention and he was discouraged from continuing. Then, around the time of independence, he had healed a man who was shot in the arm by the Indonesian military. Since then, his fame had spread through the region and he was now in demand to treat many musculoskeletal injuries. He also remains an avid cockfighter.

Senhor Januario's healing practice involved massage and the application of water infused with small fragments of 11 secret botanical species that he harvested from the forest. Januario says that his healing power came from a dream. His traditional bamboo-and-thatch 'clinic' was frequently brimming with local people who had been involved in vehicle accidents. He told us that, after a large accident in the area, it is not uncommon for *microlets* (local minivan transport) to arrive at the clinic laden with patients requesting his treatment. Even the local hospital would sometimes refer people to him rather than to the larger regional hospital. He is able to maintain his practice without any support from the formal health system.

When we arrived at his clinic, consultations on the bamboo daybed at the front of the house by the road were in full swing. Januario was massaging and gently manipulating the shoulder of a young man who had broken his arm in a motorbike accident. When the injury occurred three months ago in Dili, he had been treated there by a healer in the capital. However, the break had not mended well, and he remained in chronic pain. He had travelled the two hours from his village to see Januario. Several other inpatients of the clinic also awaited treatment. A woman who had been there for two months had sustained a serious injury on her lower leg, also from a motorbike accident. Another woman from the mountains of Matebian had broken her leg falling out of a pomelo tree. She had been in the clinic for six weeks. Shortly after we arrived, a young local girl with a broken arm walked in. 'This one broke her arm dancing,' joked Januario. It turned out she had slipped when washing the dishes at a wedding celebration.

The newest patient at the clinic that day was a young man who had arrived two days earlier with an injury to his lower leg. Januario introduced him and quickly pointed to another bamboo house next door. 'That's where his younger brother is,' he tells us. 'He has much more serious injuries.' We were taken to see the brother who lay prone on a bamboo bed. His still-bloodied lower leg was strapped with bamboo splints and tied with lengths of cloth where the tibia had snapped. 'He will need to be here for the next four months,' said Januario calmly.

The boy, Salvador, smiled at us weakly and turned down the music playing through his smartphone. He explained that two days previous he had been riding pillion on his brother's motorbike back to his village so that he could sort out his electoral card documentation. (He was planning to apply for a Portuguese passport that would allow him to work in Europe.) As they made their way up the final stretch of a windy mountain road, they found themselves head-on with a bus coming from the opposite direction. The drunk bus driver was on the wrong side of the road. On impact, Salvador's leg slammed into the steps of the bus. Salvador's family had brought him straight to Senhor Januario. No one even thought of taking him to the hospital. There, people say, such a severe injury would result in an amputation, and so it's better to keep well away.

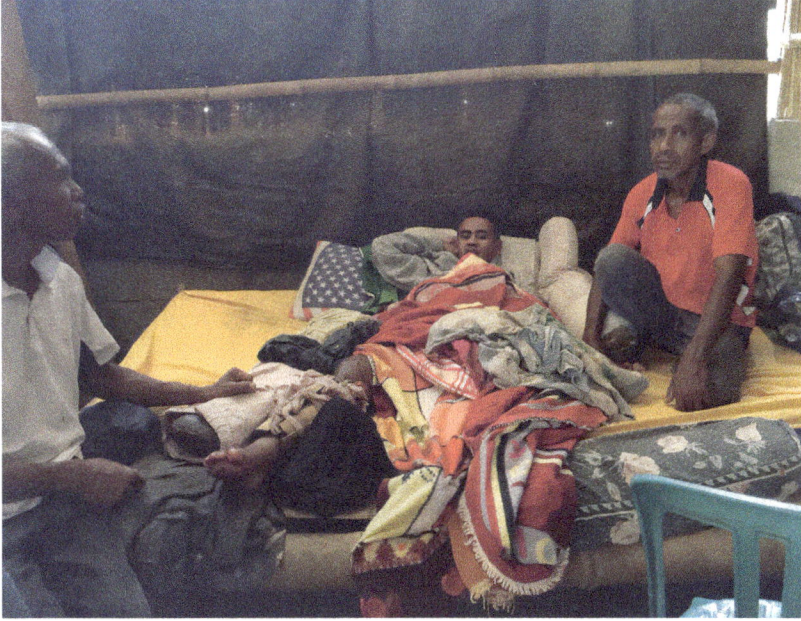

Photo 45: Januario's clinic with Salvador and his father.

The day before, the police and the owner of the bus had visited the clinic and the bus owner had promised to pay the costs of the boy's treatment, including the cost of antibiotics that Senhor Januario had sourced from contacts within the formal health system to treat infection. Salvador's father, who was sleeping by his side during the months of treatment, held great faith in Senhor Januario. 'He uses only water to treat people,' he said, to assure us that Senhor Januario was not a healer of the dark arts. Senhor Januario and his patients repeated that his treatments involved only manipulations and water. He kept a small bottle of water next to him to use as a part of the massage treatment. The seriously injured boy would have his legged unwrapped and treated regularly with this water.

Away from the clinic, other stories of Senhor Januario's healing powers and practices emerged. I was frequently told by those who know him that Januario relies on other healing powers beyond the use of water. They say his healing knowledge comes from his communication with a great snake—a snake whose life he saved and who has now bequeathed to him the knowledge of bone healing (and botanical medicine). The story goes that Senhor Januario was out with an Indonesian hunting party one day when someone in the party came across a water python and severed its body in two. Aghast at this act, Senhor Januario circled back alone to recover the two parts of the python and sew them back together. Because of this redemptive act, he now has access to the python's power.

Various villagers tell me that Januario's healing is enabled by this *dai* (nature spirit). At night-time, the water python slithers into bed with Januario's patients and wraps itself around their limbs to fuse the bones and assist Januario in the massage process. The botanical residues in the special water function to call the snake's assistance. But patients must be careful to avoid eating garlic during this treatment, they say. Garlic repels snakes.

***

On another occasion, we travelled to meet Joaquin and Palmira, a husband and wife team of healers, in a remote valley in the hinterland of Bercoli. This time I was accompanied by the director of the local health clinic. We talked about healers in the region and I asked whether or not there are any direct links between them and the formal health system. 'Not really,' he said. 'But we do encourage people to consult with customary healers according to their *fiar* (trust or belief).' He explained that in Timor-Leste there are two main types of specialist healers, with some crossover between the two. There are those who consult directly with the spirit world and then there are those who understand well the healing properties of plants. He said that the latter healers are particularly useful to know more about because they may offer an opportunity to modernise Timorese medicine. I am intrigued to learn more about how the ancient and modern might combine.

Arriving at the couple's property, we sat in the shade of their origin house. We had met Joaquin the year before at the house of my research counterpart, retired mental health nurse Senhor Almeida. Joaquin's father lived next door to Senhor Almeida in the town of Venilale. The families knew each other well and Joaquin had, at the time, successfully treated Senhor Almedia's wife for a gallstone aliment that had failed to respond to treatment at the local health clinic. Joaquin was something of a mystic healer and his healing practice was quite esoteric and, during that first meeting at least, very difficult to comprehend. His wife, Palmira, was immediately much warmer and open. After she had prepared coffee and snacks, she took us enthusiastically through many of the plant treatments she commonly uses. She explained the process of harvesting forest medicines and how she and her husband would trial these medicines and observe the effects on each other before offering such treatments to others. Given her enthusiasm, we arranged to return another day to observe her treating her patients. On the agreed day, to our surprise, she had gathered together about a dozen of her patients, most of them family, from all around the valley. Many told us they had walked hours to be there, some carrying small babies. Like Senhor Almeida's wife, most had first sought treatment unsuccessfully at the local health clinic. They clearly thought highly of Palmira and her practice.

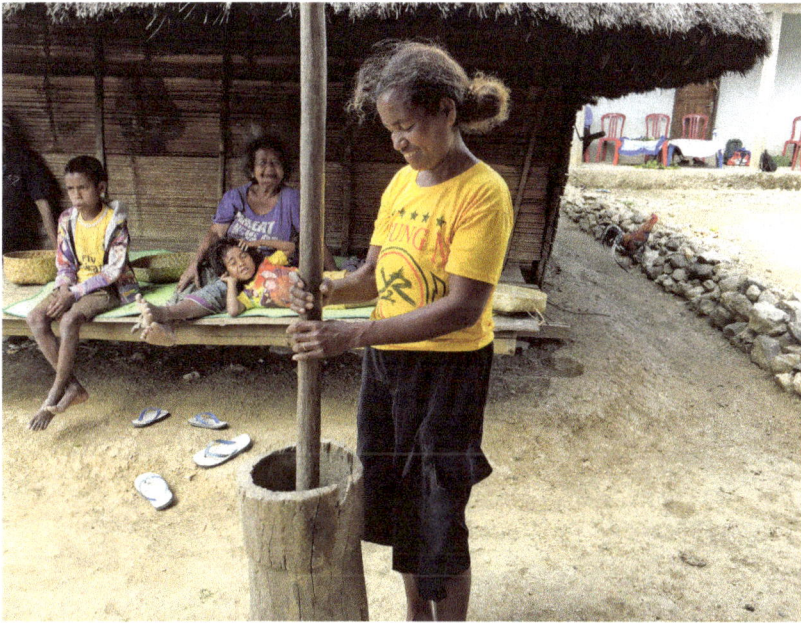

Photo 46: Palmira pounding forest medicine.

A week or so later, we headed deeper into the mountains to meet another healer reputed to be very knowledgeable about the healing properties of plants. He, like Joaquin, was also understood to heal via his intimate access to the power of nature spirits. We were accompanied once again by Senhor Almeida. Senhor Almeida is a renowned institution in the region and seemingly loved by everyone. He first learnt his nursing practice in the jungle as a resistance fighter, later returning to civilian life and dedicating his working life to healing others. He had not wanted to retire, but his hand was forced by his advancing age. The problem was that no one seemed to know or trust his replacement, and so Senhor Almeida continued to receive requests for house visits. He had, over his years of practice, cultivated both a deep respect for customary healing practices and traditions and a passion to find ways to better engage them with the formal health system.

This meeting had been set up for us by the health clinic director in a house where Senhor Almeida had never been. As we drove along the red dirt road skirting the craggy Ariana mountain ridge, the views across to the main Matebian mountain range and down the river valley across to the sea were stunning. The bamboo and concrete houses in the area were bathed in sunlight, a welcome change to the fog and damp that envelops this area for much of the year. Everything that day seemed to be sparkling, lush, cool and green. We stopped at a house for directions and were pointed towards the 'teacher's house'. The healer lived nearby.

The village was nestled amid a beautiful grove under the eastern peaks of Mount Ariana. In the 1990s, a giant statue of Our Lady had been erected on the top of the mountain. On clear days during the rice harvest season in the Wai Daba valley below, we had been able to see a gleaming white object rising up from the peak. Noyti's kids were always angling for us to drive them there so we could all climb to the top for a photo opportunity. The Old Lady was far less keen on the idea. As her own origin house hailed from this mountain area, she knew that the peaks were a site of great *lulik* power and that the statue was now interfering with their force. Why else, she argued, would the statue have been twice struck by lightning and badly damaged?

Somebody went to fetch the healer, Senhor Domingos, and when he came down to meet us he directed our vehicle up a steep narrow path where we found a house and yard full of people. Tarpaulins were draped in a marquee arrangement out the front, and many people were gathered underneath, some eating and others working on what looked to be carpentry. A monument of sorts was under construction just uphill on the other side of the house. We could also make out many more people seated inside around a long table that was covered in a *tais*. We were invited to take our place on the seating on the veranda. Many men quickly gathered to sit with us. All this activity made me think that somebody must have died, and that we had arrived during the early stages of a *mate uma* (death house). What an unfortunate time to arrive for an interview, I ruminated.

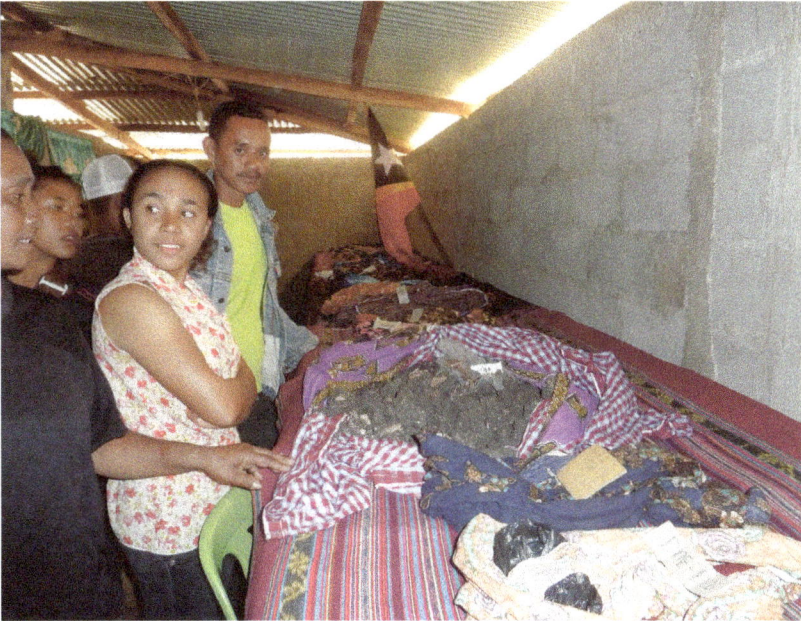

Photo 47: Collected bones and soil in their sarongs.

It soon became apparent, however, that something else was going on. On closer inspection from the veranda, I could see that there was not a coffin on the table as one would expect to find at a *mate uma*. Rather, there were a large number of bundled materials. We learned that these 23 sarongs contained the remains of this origin house's war dead. Each sarong was lain carefully along the length of the long *tais*-covered table. As we were later shown, each contained the actual bones—or rocks, as symbolic bones—of men, women and children who had died in the early years of the invasion. As the Indonesian troops took control of the area, many had fled across the valley or the relative safety of the Matebian mountains. Some were hunted and killed by the Indonesian military; others starved to death. Their bodies had never been recovered and laid to rest. Until now.

After recent consultation with the nature spirits, family members of the deceased had organised a bone-recovery party and, over a concerted two-month period, the party had followed a path down across the valley and into the forests of the Matebian range. The remains recovered on that journey had then been temporarily stored in the health clinic in the mountainous village of Kelikai. The day before our arrival, the Ministry of Health had provided an ambulance to transport the remains of the 23 deceased back to Ariana. The long journey from the Matebian mountains to the coast and back up again to Mount Ariana had taken it the best part of day.

Here at the house, they were laid out inside their sarongs on the table. As we were invited in to pay our respects, each sarong was carefully opened to reveal the name of the deceased written on a scrap of cardboard. I saw immediately that these were nearly all indigenous Timorese names; few had a Portuguese or Christian name. It was then that I understood our hosts' explanation of the scene. In two days' time, a Catholic priest would be attending the house to posthumously baptise each of these people. Their individual remains would then each be placed in the tiny chipboard coffins that many of the young men were busily making under the marquee out front. Each would be 'dressed' first, their clothes folded and placed along with their remains in the coffin. Two days later, the community would gather together in the graveyard overlooking Matebian for a full Catholic mass. A large grave with 23 separate compartments had already been prepared.

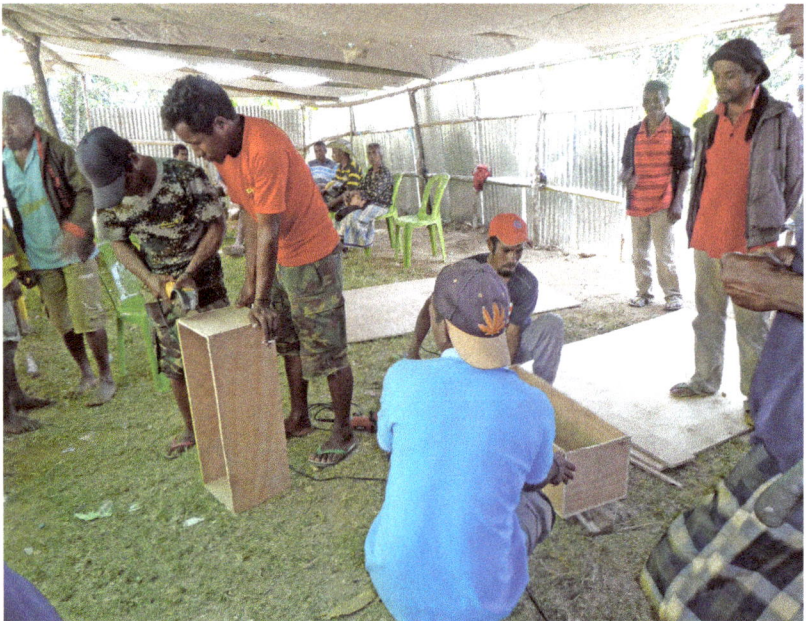

Photo 48: Making the burial coffins.

I quickly abandoned my aim of interviewing the healer and suggested to Senhor Almeida that I would be happy to record anything those assembled would like to say. I offered to video the speakers and return it as a record of their commentary and of this event. Our hosts immediately agreed. It dawned on me then the reason the health clinic director had organised for us to visit the house on this particular day. He, too, is a member of this community and it was obvious that he and his family wanted their struggle recorded. My presence to them was not an inconvenience: it offered this house a chance that their story, and their determination to properly bury their war dead, would reach the wider world.

It was a palpably emotional time for everyone assembled there. The property was crowded with people, from the infirm to newborns. I could feel the powerful aura surrounding the task at hand and the determination, no matter the circumstances, to honour and respectfully lay to rest their relatives. The monument under construction outside the house commemorated two fallen heroes: FALINTIL fighters who had died in battle. For this process, they had support through the reparations available from the government-sponsored resistance veteran's fund. But the reburial of family members—ordinary victims of war—had fallen to the survivors of the conflict. One house, comprising more than 200 people, had 25 dead bodies to lay to rest.

As we sat with the men on the veranda, I was struck with a wave of emotion and an overwhelming sadness. I was not sure if I could go through with the interview. But this sorrow derives, in part, from somewhere else; it trains its wrath on the world that I customarily inhabit and that grants me great privileges. Here we were in an obviously impoverished community who were coming together to try to recover from the ravages of a period of war waged more than 40 years ago. My own country had covertly provoked and supported the invasion and occupation of East Timor. The guns used by the soldiers and the bombs dropped on this region were dropped by planes supplied by the US and UK governments, Australia's allies. Now, these distant Western powers congratulate themselves on overseeing Timor-Leste's independence and status as a new nation-state. At the same time, they increasingly express their exasperation at the lack of Timorese 'development' and capacity. Yet the people affected by these bloody campaigns continue to draw on their collective cultural capacity to try to deal with their loss and trauma and to move forward in the most intimate and physically connected way possible. Their everyday lives are a world away from the boardrooms where development experts seek advice on overcoming 'cultural barriers' to development.

I knew that I must push my emotions aside and recover my composure from the shock of this visceral and unexpected encounter with a 'post-conflict community' so as to begin the video recording. Once the camera was rolling, I could better appreciate the greater significance of the event. Far from being backward-looking, the intention is firmly trained on ensuring the prosperity and pathways of current and future generations. I realised, too, that although we would not be carrying out the expected interview with a 'healer', this event and recorded commentary were entirely about health and healing.

The burial of these physical remains is not the end of the journey. Rather, it opens a path forward into the future. It gives the living a way to continue with their own lives. As usual, the main concern was marriage relations between houses. Enabling and properly negotiating their own marriage arrangements would not be possible until the death arrangements of their parents and grandparents had been properly concluded. The exchanges between houses that surround a death ritual act to settle outstanding debts, to brings past events to a close at the same time as they create new paths and openings. But all of this requires a body to collectively grieve over and lay to rest. This process had not been possible. Until now.

The few days before the bodies were to be posthumously christened and then buried was especially important. After Senhor Almeida had presciently raised the topic, it was explained to me, on camera, that the family members of this and associated houses would come together and negotiate the past marriage arrangements of the deceased and settle any outstanding debts as a part of their burial. These exchanges, once concluded, would allow the deceased to transition out of the darkness and into the light. Catholic christening would also lead them to the light and was in accordance with contemporary societal expectations. Most importantly, in the next year's consecration of corn and rice following harvest, the deceased would take up their rightful places as the protectors of the living. Once properly buried, the names of the deceased can be called out at these annual agricultural rituals. They would be honoured as ancestors and asked to give their blessing and support to the living. Their spirits would now reside inside the house, the physical structure of which was located up the hill in the mountain peaks.

Photo 49: The 23 grave compartments.

Senhor Domingos, the healer, explained that the time before the priest's arrival were critical hours for the families to sit in communication with their loved ones. They would sit together 'in the darkness' and journey together through the ritual process that is required by the spirit realm. 'Then,' he said, 'we will hand them over to the priest for the next stage in their journey.'

Later, I told this story to Louisa, a sister-in-law in Baucau, and she was overcome by sadness for her own reasons. As a young child, Louisa, her mother and her baby sister had lived in the forests on the run for more than a year following the Indonesian invasions. Louisa's father had only managed to find them after he joined the Indonesian army as a porter. During their forest patrols, he used the opportunity to call out to his wife in Makasae. By some miracle, as his wife and children huddled together close to starvation in a small, forested cave, they heard him call to them and surrendered. Other family members were not so lucky. Many of their extended family died during this time. Their bodies had never been recovered. 'We didn't even find one,' she said, choking back tears. Across the country, similar bone-recovery and reburial processes have been completed or are underway. It is a process of intergenerational healing in which some have more success than others.

On that day in Ariana, we wrapped up the commentary and filming of the process quite quickly and said our goodbyes. I felt rushed, but Quin was keen to leave. He had his own death business to attend to. An old man in the village had died and we had promised our family we would be back in time to join them in the visit to the *mate uma*.

On return to Bercoli, we gathered at one of the uncle's houses before travelling in convoy to the house of the deceased. We drove to the funeral with the back part of our car crammed full of young nieces and nephews. Quin called out to them that there was a competition to see who the best wailer was today. Our kids and I weren't sure if he was teasing or not. We unloaded our gifts—several sacks of rice, slabs of sweet drinks and carefully folded piles of *tais*—and were ushered into the front room of the tiny mud-floored house. The *tais* were added to the collection alongside of the coffin. The aunties and other older women in our group began the vigorous *halele* (ritual wail) over the coffin. With the release of this guttural wailing there was a surge of emotion in the room. Although they had participated in many such funerals, Madalena and Zeca looked disconcerted. It had been a strange day and it was humid and very hot in the small coffin-filled room. Our bodies were pressed tightly together and the smell of the deceased wafting from the coffin was overpowering. The wailing continued for some time as the others of us stood together and silently paid our respects. I comforted Zeca that we would soon be leaving, but then another party of mourners arrived and somehow squeezed into the room with us. The older women in this party did not take part in the *halele*. While some of the women from our party continuing to wail, the newcomers began instead to recite the rosary. All the other members of their party and the non-wailing members of our party joined in. It was both soothing and bedlam. Rosary prayers alternated with hymns. This seemed to go on forever and Zeca slipped away to play with the younger boys outside. Madalena was by then squashed deep in the far corner of the room with her girl cousins and couldn't move. Quin quipped later that we were lucky it was only five rounds of the rosary, not 10. Finally, silence descended, and we were all ushered out of the room so that other newly arrived groups of mourners could take our place.

We sat and chatted with fellow groups of mourners gathered outside before our group was escorted to the house next door. There, a marquee was erected, and dozens of large plates of meat were laid on the table. I noticed the many pigs, goats, horses and buffalo in the yards surrounding the property, and the makeshift kitchen full of people where the freshly slaughtered meat was being carved up. But it was not yet time to for our party to eat. The meat laid out on the table was pork for the *fetosaa* (fertility-taker) in-laws. After that, the goat and buffalo meat would be laid out for the *umane* (fertility-giver) in-laws. We were considered part of the house so we would eat last. We were asked to take refreshments in another area where the table was laid out with sweet drinks and cake. We were then ushered out again shortly after so the next party could take their seats and refreshments. While we waited for our meal to be served, we were asked to sit with the Old Man and some of the other senior men from the household and village. Others in our party went to help in the kitchen.

One of the men seated with us, Joao, was a catechist, the younger brother of the deceased. Presumably for the benefit of us as outsiders, people known to frown on the extravagance of Timorese death rituals, Joao noted disapprovingly that:

> It is too much. There is the *mate uma* (death house ritual), the *ai funan moruk* and *midar* (two separate sweet and bitter flower rituals), the *kore metan* (end of mourning ritual) and then they open it all up again two or three years later for another final ritual. It should just be one ritual involving prayers from the priest. Our Timorese identity is linked to our houses and our agricultural rituals. Death should be left to the church.

From their muted reaction, it appeared that the other men seated with us did not agree, although they didn't say much at the time. Later, back at home, the Old Man told us that he and the others had spent the rest of the afternoon negotiating the outstanding debts of the houses linked to the deceased. One reason for this was that the mother of the deceased (who was also the mother of Joao, the catechist) had been buried several decades ago without rituals, negotiations or complicated exchanges. Because she had died during the early years of the Indonesian invasion, the people had simply returned to the village from the mountains, and the priest had given a simple blessing and that was all. But, as the Old Man said: 'That was then, and this is now'. With the death of her son, protocol and the health of future generations demanded that the negotiations held off during the war be reopened. The deceased's mother's business must be fully settled before they could properly bury her son and negotiate the outstanding arrangements between the various houses involved. Exchanges must be organised and gifted to the mother's family by her deceased husband and son's house before they could bury and talk about the processes involved in her son's funerary proceedings. The Old Man observed that Joao had looked very glum during the protracted negotiations. 'But he didn't say anything. These practices are our law.'

One day, two sets of ostensibly different death rituals. Yet what had transpired at the *mate uma* was essentially the same as what was occurring at the *haloot ruin* (bone-recovery ritual) in the mountains earlier in the day. The time elapsed since death and the presence of actual bodies may have varied, but both rituals were about ensuring that familial relations were in order, and that the pathways to healing were opened up so that the names of the dead could be properly honoured, and societal relations could continue to unfold.

13

New Beginnings

A few days later, I went with the Old Man to another Bercoli 'repair' project on the drylands of the plateau. This time the task concerned the rebuilding of a complex of six origin houses that had all been burnt down in the early years of the Indonesian occupation. Much of the houses' ancestral heirlooms had also been lost in these fires or through subsequent displacements. Now, finally, the families involved had amassed the resources and momentum necessary to rebuild. All six houses would be rebuilt over the coming 12 months. The *hatama ai* (carrying in of the wood) ceremony signalled the formal commencement of the reconstruction.

I had been to many house rebuilding ceremonies, but I was not prepared for the scale of this undertaking. We arrived to find piles and piles of hand-cut and carefully stacked timbers, several hundred metres of stacked grasses and black palm fibres for use in thatching and rope making, countless lengths of bamboo used to construct temporary kitchens and living shelters, stacks of wood for the kitchen fires, huge pots for cooking the rice and stews, and many livestock tethered around the perimeter. Local *microlets* were continually arriving with locally sourced supplies. Some had huge bunches of green bananas tied to their roof. These would later be boiled and used as a high energy snack. Even more impressive were the hundreds of people—house members, their extended families and in-laws—gathered to help with the various activities of the build: to move materials, to make ropes, to cook, to carry water, to slaughter animals, to wash dishes, to serve food, to guard the sacra, to dispense the sacred betel, to sit and talk and bring to life the stories of the houses and, most importantly of all, to carry out exchanges that would carry forward the lives and relationships of all of those attached to these houses. It was awe-inspiring to witness.

Photo 50: Carrying the grasses into the house reconstruction site.

The Old Man was in charge of the operation. Although not technically from the house complex, he was a close cousin from an important and aligned house. He led the discussions around the ritual organisation. His job was to 'speak' on behalf of the senior house members, to talk through the obligations and responsibilities of the parties for the rebuild and especially to negotiate their exchanges with their in-law houses. On this day, it appeared that there was little need for extended discussion. All had been prepared and everything was working like clockwork. The people gathered knew, based on their particular relations to the house, what their roles were. The varied tasks involved in the reconstruction were not dissimilar to other life cycle events, although the rebuilding of six sacred houses was clearly a demanding logistical feat. The largest house in the complex was to be rebuilt right on the edge of the plateau to face directly across the valley to the mountains of Matebian. Perched splendidly on the cliffs, this was to be the parent house of the other five 'child' houses.

There were around 50 households belonging to these six houses and another 63 houses were associated with the build as in-law houses. The sheer number of people involved, and the requirement that they attend and bring gifts, created a long-term reciprocal burden for the members of the reconstructed house complex. As these in-law houses arrived at the house during the period of reconstruction, they brought with them gifts of buffalo, horses, goats, and ceremonial swords. At crucial points in the future, the hosts would be required to reciprocate with return gifts of pigs, woven cloth, rice, palm wine and other drinks.

Photo 51: The parent house reconstruction site with Matebian mountains in the background.

The reconstruction process had already been underway for three months. The first month had been spent discussing the process, and two months had been spent in the surrounding region collecting the materials, including grasses, palm fibres and timber, and preparing the site. Temporary structures had been constructed to house and feed the throngs of participants. So far, four of the goats brought as gifts by the in-laws had been sacrificed for the grass-collection, along with two buffalo and a horse for the *hatama ai* ceremony.

The ceremony involved moving by hand the collected materials from their main storage site to the house complex site a hundred or so metres away. The site was inside the *lulik* zone, a place also peppered with large sacred limestone megaliths. Only those in the appropriate relationships to the house complex were permitted to carry in the materials. A specialist house builder from the local area had been secured to oversee the build, a process that was estimated would take a year or more. Dozens of the house members would remain onsite to assist the specialist. Hundreds more people would reconvene in a year's time to complete the *suku uma*, the final stage of thatching.

The houses were to be constructed only from natural materials, without metal or nails. A critically important job for the large numbers of men gathered was to make the black palm–fibre ropes. Like the relations that bind peoples together, so these ropes would materially bind together and reinforce the structure of the house. The element binding the houses to the ancestral world was water. The house complex was associated with the nearby spring of Wai Dasu (Dog Water). For all important rituals, the women connected to the house complex would walk the 30 minutes or so to draw spring water for use in the ritual blessings required to enliven and cleanse the houses, their sacred objects and people.

I learnt, however, that there was a crucial gap in the relations and contributions considered necessary to enable the reconstruction. Speaking to the camera, the senior custodian expressed his sadness that one group had not come to the party. A large church-run technical and agricultural college nearby also drew its daily water supply from Wai Dasu. Indeed, the land on which the college was built in the Portuguese colonial period was gifted to the church by this origin house and the associated village. The villagers had even helped build the college itself. I knew, from conversations with the Old Man, that this history was continually invoked by the elders in their discussions over the processes needed to rebuild the house complex. From their perspective, the college should also have been actively contributing to the rebuilding process. Yet when the elders had made a formal request to the college leadership, the priests maintained that they only had resources to help out with the building of churches, not origin houses.

The rebuild was expensive, both in time and resources. Ancestral heirlooms had been lost or looted in the chaos of the Indonesian era and these items must somehow be recovered. House members had been working on this project over many years, searching to find local artisans from whom they could secure replicas. Even so, the process was fraught and time consuming. The recrafted objects needed to be identical to the lost items, details of which were often sketchy. Complicated ritual processes were involved to ensure that the new objects would be correctly inspirited. A sword is not just a sword; it must be infused with the personhood attached to the original object.

After I had filmed the *hatama ai* ceremony, a senior house custodian took me to a temporary bamboo shelter that represented the parent house and that contained the rocks of the sacred hearth. Inside sat an elderly woman and her husband who were charged with guarding the amassed objects. The woman explained that it was her job throughout the rebuilding of this house to tend the sacred hearth. Her husband's job was to dispense the betel leaf, at critical junctures, from the house's sacred hearth to all of those participating in the ceremony.

Photo 52: Offerings to the sacra.

The shelter was also a gathering point for other senior house members, including the Old Man. There they chatted, rested, organised, told house histories and other stories from the past. While they sat there, some of their grandchildren would drift in and out. So, too, did the daughters of the house who had married out and whose families were now the bringers of buffalo and horses and swords so essential to the ceremony. Inside, on a raised bamboo platform, were many metal and wooden chests filled with the sacred objects to be distributed between the six houses. The chests contained clothing, *tais*, metal breast plates and headpieces, most of which had been recently acquired. These objects were now, in communication with the ancestral realm, going through a process of inspiriting. All food cooked on the sacred hearth would first be placed on plates in front of each of the chests, as offerings to the ancestors of the houses who were now actively re-inspiriting the objects.

Below the bamboo platform, there hung 20 or more swords that had been gifted by various in-law houses. These would later be passed to the child houses whose job it was to provide spiritual security to the parent house. There were baskets of *tais* that would be used as return gifts to the in-law houses. A red rooster was tethered permanently by the shelter's entrance, just as each house would eventually have a red rooster permanently at its door. This is *lulik*.

As we sat and chatted, one of the elders began to recount, for the benefit of the camera, one of the founding stories of the house. It was a story of connection between this dryland house and an origin house on the escarpment edge closer to Baucau and the coast. It turned out to be a direct counterpart to one I had heard many years before at the other house. The story involved members of the two houses encountering one another and exchanging knowledge of fire and water, and their ensuing misadventures. In both versions of the story, the defining characteristic of the characters involved was that their mouths were full of hair. According to the now deceased Major Ko'o Raku, this feature indicated that they were *Butu*, a first people of the region who were descended from colonies of termites.

The people of the plateau were pleased when I told them that I had heard the paired version of this story from the house closer to the coast. 'You need to write this all down and bring us back that story and our story in a book,' they said. I asked tentatively if they might not prefer that I bring them the film I was recording. After all, I said, it would contain the images of the elders recounting the story directly in your own words. Yes, of course they said, the film would be nice. But they made it clear, what they really wanted was the book. 'We want to put it in our origin house,' said the senior custodian. 'This will help us to replace the book we lost when our houses were burnt down. That book also contained our history.' On further questioning, it turned out that this burnt book was a book of early twentieth-century tax receipts, much like the book that was lost when the Old Man's Wai Daba house was burnt down. Such books are tangible power objects. In their various manifestations they are used to honour and to prove connections to and responsibilities for a place.

The Old Man had also frequently told me to write a book for him telling the story of Wai Daba and its pivotal role in the Bercoli kingdom. The Wai Daba house is also yet to be rebuilt. When it is, the senior members of the house complex currently being reconstructed said they would be there to 'speak' on his behalf and to reciprocate his services. They will negotiate the law and the exchanges of gifts between the Wai Daba and its in-law houses. 'We are family of sorts with the Old Man,' they tell me. 'When he rebuilds his house, it will be our job to help him build community.'

Quin and I had long been talking with the Old Man about building our own house in Bercoli. Over the years, he had taken us to several sites that he deemed appropriate. Over time, I realised that each of these locations foregrounded the 'repair' of the Wai Daba estate, a house with extensive customary lands and responsibilities, though with relatively few people. The Old Man carefully gave us options, but left the final choice to us. We strongly favoured a site cradled in the valley of the rice fields. After working the harvest, we felt invested in this place. This was also the valley where many of Quin's ancestors had lived until the Indonesian era had forced people's habitations closer to the roads. The foundations of their houses still lay crumbling in the undergrowth, and the Old Man constantly recounted their stories whenever we were in the vicinity.

But there was another site that the Old Man was especially keen we visit. To get there, we travelled for two hours by car across the drylands of the plateau and down almost impassable tracks into the far western valley, to the furthest extent of the current Wai Daba estate. This spring-fed valley and its associated savannah landscape was once the beloved pastoral domain of the Old Man's uncles, prized grasslands where they had grazed their buffalo, cattle and horses. A few people still lived there, although none directly connected to the house. Few grazing animals remained. The spring-fed rice fields belonging to the Wai Daba house in this area had long been abandoned, the terraces now largely reclaimed by the forest.

We visited a family living near the site of the old residence and acting as the area's caretakers. They kept a few animals and grew some rice. The old woman and her younger brother who lived there made a living digging wild tubers from the ground. These tubers were cut into round chips and sun-dried before being onsold to merchant middlemen. People have told me they end up in China where they are somehow used in cosmetics.

As we travelled through the area with the Old Man and another uncle, Tiu Juliao, people would frequently rush from their tiny thatched houses, calling out to us with tears brimming in their eyes. The tears were for the sight of the Old Man and his brother. That these senior customary figures, people they referred to locally as royalty, had returned to visit meant a great deal to them. The visit was equally meaningful for the two brothers. Both they, and the people who now cared for these lands, expressed their love for the landscape and their sadness about the reforestation that had occurred in the area since the war. In the absence of people and grazing animals, the grasslands had disappeared. Forest was repossessing its space.

Photo 53: The Old Man walking through rice fields.

While the people of the Wai Daba house were no longer present, it was made clear to us that the spirits of the land were sentient. We were told that their ancestral names were still called out by the local people remaining there. The Old Man feared, though, that the Wai Daba spirits were angry that their families were now so far away. He encouraged Quin to buy a tractor so that he could become a sharecropper with the caretakers living on the site. 'Together,' he said, 'we can restore and till these rice fields again.' Tiu Juliao spoke of plans to rebuild a house in the area and restock the herds of cattle and horses. The pull of the remote grasslands was strong, as was the urge to reoccupy it. Besides, leaving land empty is risky; there is no telling how abandoned ancestors will respond.

The fears brought about by wildness and an absence of people were not present back in the valley where we eventually decided to build our house. There, the Wai Daba descendants engaged with the ancestral realm in their daily activities. Even so, we were building a residence in a land that had mostly been vacated of houses. The process of reoccupation needed to be carried out very carefully. Initially, we had wanted to build a traditional style of house with the roof made from black palm fibre. When we suggested this to the Old Man, he obfuscated and appeared to change the subject. He made some reference to the need to first secure the Wai Daba spring. Later, another of his younger brothers, Tiu Vicente, was more direct. 'Are you mad?' he exclaimed. 'You can't use palm fibres to build anything here until the Wai Daba origin house has been rebuilt. Unless you want us all to die straight away.' Now we understood. The Old Man could not say so much directly, but he was clearly indicating the complication of the unbuilt origin house by the Wai Daba spring. When it finally materialised, this rebuilding process would be done on a grand style befitting the regional importance of the Wai Daba house. But such a process cannot be spoken about openly, at least not by the Old Man. To speak would mean action must immediately follow. To speak and not act would be to invite retribution. So, the Old Man must be seen to hold silent, while at the same time finding subtle ways to inch forward with the complex intra- and inter-house negotiations necessary to bring this reconstruction to fruition. This is a delicate balancing act. The successful completion of the six houses on the plateau was a crucial step. In the meantime, for us to build our house with a traditional palm-fibre thatch would be a grave insult to the ancestors. We hurriedly changed our plans.

While the building of our house would commence in earnest after we had left Timor-Leste, the Old Man needed to consult the ancestors before our departure. They agreed that for the construction we could use water from the paired Wai Daba spring of Ocabai. When the Old Man eventually took us on the walk through the dense spring grove to show us where we could pipe the water, something uncanny occurred. A huge swarm of bees emerged suddenly from the hollow of a large tree by the spring lake where we were standing. 'Stay still,' hissed the Old Man. We froze. I tried to stay calm, remembering how that strategy had worked during honey harvest in Lookeu. Sure enough, the bees dissipated. I was not sure what it would have meant if they had not. The Old Man wouldn't be drawn on the significance of their appearance, but we could feel its power. He told us that once the house was ready, there would need to be a proper ceremony at the spring and a buffalo or goat would need to be offered before we could pipe the water for everyday use. In the meantime, he asked us for US$10 so he could purchase the rooster that would need to be sacrificed to the land spirits before we could break the soil at the site.

As we prepared to leave Bercoli, we were immersed in the building logistics with a local architect friend and family members. Meanwhile, the Old Man was always out in the fields. True to habit, he would walk around the valley tending to his animals and surveying the area. Yet on these days he was also quietly working on our behalf, organising a range of other matters associated with the build. This process mainly involved quietly informing and negotiating with various neighbours with whom we would share boundaries or who owned the trees that would need to be felled to build the road in. While he owned the land, many of the fruiting trees belonged to others who would need to be compensated for their loss. A coconut tree could be felled for around US$15, after which the fruit belonged to the owner and the timber to us. Much of it was used for the internal framing of the house. The Old Man also organised the younger men of the area to collect the rocks for use in the house foundations. I was not sure where these rocks were coming from, but I strongly suspected that there would be a story as to how they were chosen. Two worlds of planning and negotiation were running in parallel.

In building our own house, we were self-consciously integrating ourselves and extending our relations with Quin's living relatives and the ancestral realm. We were no longer simply visiting relatives being shaded by the Wai Daba house. Now, in a very public way, we were rooting ourselves in this place and taking on significant obligations and responsibilities, the extent of which we could neither fully imagine nor control. While the family were quietly disappointed we were not building a high status *uma andar* (concrete two-storey house), everybody appreciated our commitment and it seemed to be the talk of the bi-weekly Bercoli market place. We would not own this land in any Western sense of land tenure. We could build there only because others had authorised it, and because they will continue to negotiate with a whole range of actors on our behalf. Without such negotiation, none of it would have been possible.

Epilogue

In many ways, the themes that animate this book—those of family and kinship, wild spirits and ancestors, development, tradition and modernity— remain as relevant to our lives on the outside as they remain for those inside Timor-Leste. These threads form the wider cloth from which Timorese people's worlds, and our own, are continually woven and brought into being. Across the island, people are always attuned to the flows between diverse and disparate forms of life, ways to honour family collectivities and to find new pathways for incorporating others. The flows and communications between people, other beings and things across time and place open up spaces for the creation and negotiation of these worlds. People are also attuned to the theatrics that infuse the politics of development and new nation building, processes about and through which they are in continual multisensory and often lively conversation. During a visit to Timor-Leste in late 2019, the monsoonal rains hadn't yet come and wherever we went in the east we heard a common explanation: the Chinese companies contracted by the government to build the multimillion-dollar roads under construction had been counter-seeding the clouds, ensuring the rains would hold off so they could get their roads built and contracts fulfilled. The various actors and agencies brought into causal relationship through these conversations are rooted in particular understandings of the world and are, for outsiders, often surprising. Very often, they also reveal deep insights into variously entangled micro and macro processes.

***

It's late 2020 and I am at home in Melbourne with Quin and the kids. The year 2020 began for us with the required house-warming party in Bercoli. We had just settled into the new house and had completed connecting the water supply to the outdoor kitchen and bathroom. It was time to hold the final ceremony to ask the spirits of the Ocabai spring, from where the water was pumped, for permission to permanently use this water and to bless the house.

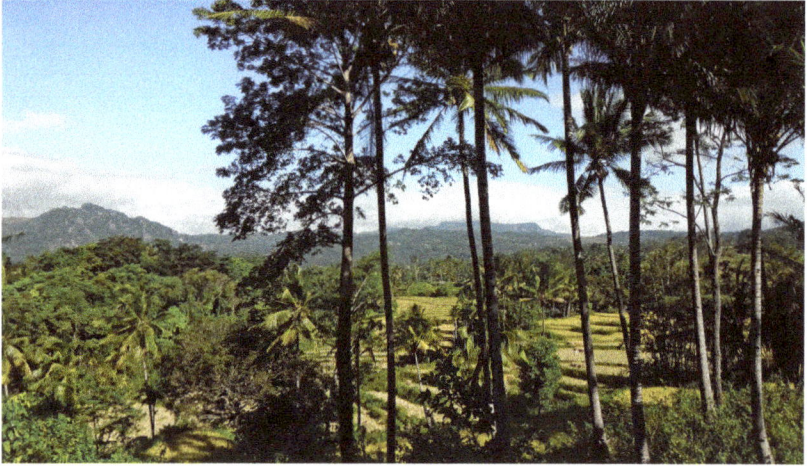

Photo 54: View from our house.
Source: Susanna Barnes.

On the day of the ceremony, the extended family from up on the main road begin to drift down. Two nieces brought with them huge cauldrons for cooking and a large wooden and metal scraping instrument for grating coconut flesh. To please the kids and in a break from tradition, we would also make *katupa* for the ceremony feast—rice cooked with spiced coconut milk in palm-sized woven baskets. The *katupa* cases had been made the day before by the kids and their cousins from the fronds of the coconut palms that fringe the house.

Eventually almost everyone had arrived. The house was alive with activity. Tia Martina's husband Tiu Antonio had brought along his beloved black dog, Captain, and our dog, Golden, spent most of the day trying to fend off his assaults. Zeca took shelter with him in one of the bedrooms.

We had secured a medium-sized goat for the offering at Ocabai. The ceremony would take place at the spring's source around half a kilometre away, through a dense palm grove and up past the bee tree. While the women of the family prepared the *katupa* spices in the kitchen, Tiu Vicente (the Old Man's chief ritual assistant on such occasions) took a snippet of the goat's fur, a red rooster, betel nut and 12 coins (five plus seven) with him to the spring. When the Old Man rose to go with him, I made a move to follow with the video camera. The Old Man stopped me in my tracks. '*Feto sira la bele ba*' ['Women can't go'], he said quietly. I was getting used to this by now and I gave the camera to Quin, asked him to film the ceremony and headed back to the kitchen.

Photo 55: Cooking *katupa* by the kitchen.

The men followed the water channel upstream and placed the coins and betel nut by an altar at the spring source, circling the chicken five and seven times in the air. The Old Man made a prayer and asked for the blessings from the ancestors of the spring and associated Wai Daba origin house. By the time they returned to our house, the goat had been slaughtered and I was called from the kitchen to resume filming. The Old Man read the liver of the slaughtered goat. 'All is good,' he told me quietly, 'although the ancestors are little angry.' When I asked tentatively why this might be so, he said that Quin had been speaking out of turn. In recent days he had been badgering the Old Man and his brothers about when they were going to begin the reconstruction of the Wai Daba origin house. This had upset the Old Man and, it seemed, the ancestors. To speak on such matters so openly and within the domain of the rice fields meant that the reconstruction must begin immediately. As this was impossible, the ancestors were angered by the empty words. The Old Man made it clear they would need to be placated with the appropriate offerings at the next harvest ritual. The same message of displeasure showed up next in the Old Man's reading of the sacrificed red rooster's liver. When I relayed this message to Quin he dismissed it breezily. 'The ancestors are happy that I am bringing these things up and moving them forward,' he shot back. Thankfully the reading of the final liver, that of the white chicken, indicated that all was in order with our new house and its water supply.

Photo 56: The Old Man carrying out a ritual at the Ocabai spring source.

Once the goat meat and rice were placed in bamboo lengths and cooked over the fire, certain portions were carried back to the spring for a final offering. On their return to the house, the brothers and Quin were joined by another relative, Achilles, and the four of them travelled along a route that took in a large rectangular perimeter of the forest-fringed house site. Achilles, one of the members of a newcomer family who is always faithful to the authority of the Old Man, placed offerings of the cooked meat and rice in each corner of the perimeter and finally in a central location in front of the house. This ensured that the ancestral spirits would both observe and maintain a border between the wild spirit world and our everyday living space.

When they arrived back to the house, I was again called from the kitchen to take over filming. The blood of the sacrificed white chicken was tipped into a freshly picked coconut, and the mixture of blood and coconut water was sprinkled by Achilles inside the house and around the garden. The coconut was then placed upturned on a log sticking up at the front of the house—a signal to all passers-by that the house was now properly blessed and protected. With the ritual proceedings now over, it was time for us to eat, drink and celebrate the end to a more than year-long construction. Concerned perhaps for my foreign predispositions, one of Tia Martina's daughters who was recently returned from studying in Dili took me aside quietly and suggested it might have been better if we had had a Catholic priest bless the house. I don't think she was sure what to make of me when I replied that such a priest might not be powerful enough for the task at hand.

Before he left that evening, Quin had told the Old Man I would be going to Portugal for a conference later in the year. 'Be sure to bring back that book of our tax records,' he reminded me sternly. This led in turn to another lengthy conversation with the other men present about what could be done about those others who were, in his view, intent on surreptitiously claiming parts of the valley as their own inheritance.

***

I never did get to Portugal in 2020. Not long after we arrived back in Australia coronavirus emerged as a global pandemic and we pretty much stayed at home in Melbourne for the remainder of the year.

Often in the evenings around dinner time, Quin would sit at the dining table making phone calls to Timor to catch up on all the family news. In the beginning we were all very worried about the potential impact of COVID-19 in Timor-Leste. Early on the government closed the country's borders and declared a state of emergency. As Timorese frequently do when they sense trouble, many left the capital just before a state of emergency was declared and returned to their home villages. Across the country, including at the Wai Daba spring, the *lia na'in* held ritual ceremonies to ask the ancestors for their assistance in combating COVID-19. These ceremonies were posted on social media and shared among families inside and outside Timor-Leste. The *lia na'in* addressed the disease as a living being and implored it not to travel to Timor-Leste.

Months later, the virus had yet to emerge outside of Dili, and while life in the capital was badly affected by the stay-at-home orders, in Bercoli, where people had access to their fields and a diversity of cultivated and wild foods, life went on as normal. One day, we called Tia Martina to ask how she was going. In 2019, her oldest daughter had left the village to work in England. The daughter's husband, who was from elsewhere in Timor-Leste, had been working there in a factory for many years. Tia Martina was then left to care for three young grandchildren and, although she did not complain, it significantly added to the burden of her daily household and agricultural tasks. We wanted to know how the young couple were going in England and whether they had been able to keep their jobs during the pandemic. Pleased we had called her to check in, Tia Martina exchanged pleasantries (which in these contexts take the form of much teasing) and then told us what she really thought of the current situation. While the incomes of those lucky enough to have a job in Dili and the remittances from those working overseas were highly valued and appreciated, what people in the village objected to was the sheer mass of underemployed youth who now resided in the capital. Tia Martina said that it was now clear, more than ever, that these largely idle youth needed to return permanently to the villages to help their families with the agricultural work and other household tasks.

Other than that, as had been the case in late 2019, her main concern remained the rain. The season's rains had eventually arrived, but they were very late, delaying the sowing of staple crops. Tia Martina said she didn't remember the rains being this late before. Then, towards the end of the severely delayed rainy season, widespread flooding affected much of the country. In badly affected regions, people had needed to rely on emergency food aid and international assistance.

These rural happenings reflect the paradox of development in Timor-Leste. While the local customary communities can often rely on their own strength and resilience to get them through tough times, increasingly extreme climate events and unexpected global shocks such as the COVID-19 pandemic create deeper global entanglements that, in different ways, shape and contest both the promises of development and the implications of its underdevelopment.

***

The worry about COVID-19 soon passed from them to us. A second-wave surge of the virus in Melbourne meant that we remained in lockdown. Meanwhile, across Timor it was wedding season. Quin's nightly conversations turned to the customary negotiations around all the marriages being negotiated across the family network. Quin, who is always far less interested in all these details than me, would reluctantly engage in the banter, putting the phone on speaker so I could hear, too. Listening on the phone to various conversations about these often geographically far-flung marriages of the next generation of nieces and nephews, who was giving what, who withheld what, I am continually struck by these impressive feats of customary accounting and the associated flow charts.

Marriage practices may be changing, but they are still made legible and writ large through the customary machinations of extended family politics—machinations in which we, much to Quin's consternation, were increasingly expected to play a part. While we were a long way from family, I was reminded of the fact that culture in Timor-Leste also has the knack of working its way from the inside out.

Many of these telephone conversations were between Quin and Tiu Juliao, the Old Man's younger brother. The Old Man himself tends to leave these cross-island marriage negotiations concerning the Dili-based educated nieces and nephews to be overseen by this younger brother. Juliao is a relatively wealthy businessman in Dili and he is well connected to a certain strata of Dili society. It is always him, I notice, who steps to the fore when negotiations occur around these more 'modern' marriages. The Old Man reserves his skills for the more intense ritual negotiations of the village domain.

Later in September we spoke to the Old Man and he remained very concerned about the global COVID-19 pandemic and the situation in Melbourne. He reminded us about the efficacy of the ceremonies he carried out by the spring to ward off the virus and reflected on the power of the Wai Daba ancestors. 'You lot take care of yourselves over there,' he said, with deep concern for those living away from the hard-won protection of the ancestral hearth. We, meanwhile, look forward to our return.

Glossary of Language and Terms

Tetum unless otherwise noted.

abut laran	inside the roots
ai funan moruk, ai funan midar	two separate sweet and bitter flower funerary rituals
avo	grandparent; estuarine crocodile
bee na'in	water custodians
belak	metal breast plate/disc
bibi	goat
biru	malevolent spirit
boy fatin	swing place
chefe	head/leader
CNRT	East Timorese Political Party
dai (Waima'a, Makasae)	nature spirit, foreigner, outsider
dato	local ruler
FALINTIL	East Timorese resistance guerrillas
falun	wrapped
fanu bei-ala sira	to wake up the ancestors
fetosaa	fertility-takers
fiar	trust or belief
fo folin	to give value
fo han	to feed
FRETILIN	East Timorese political party

halele	to ritually wail
haloot ruin	bone-recovery ritual
hamlaha	hungry
hatama ai	carrying in of the wood ceremony
hun no dikin	base/trunk and tip
kaben ho lafaek	marrying with crocodiles
kabu bee	water controller, water keeper
kase (Baikeno)	foreigners/outsiders
katupa	spiced coconut cakes
kesi ema	bind people
kore metan	end of mourning ritual
kuda	horse; to plant
laku	Asian palm civet cat
lao ho liman mamuk	walk country with empty hands
lao rai sira	travellers
lia na'in	custodian of the words
liman midar	sweet hands
lipa	sarong
liu husi kotuk	exit through the back
liurai	king
lulik	ancestral potency, forbidden, sacred, taboo
lulik malu	forbidden to each other
malae	foreigner, outsider, nature spirit
matak malirin	greening coolness, life flourishing
matan dook	one who sees far, soothsayer
mate uma	death house
merah putih (Indonesian)	red and white
microlet	local minibus
morten	red coral bead necklace
piku	palm-stalk panelling
povu	the people

povu kuda, governu sosa/sae	the people grow crops, the government buys/the people are the horses, the government ride them
rai salaen (Tetum Terik)	the land is hungry
RENETIL	East Timorese student resistance organisation
sabao	type of pygeum tree
saur haree	new rice consecration ceremony
sira fiar an	believe in themselves
subar	to hide
suku uma	ceremony to finish (sew together) the origin house
tais	woven cloth
talibere	python
tama	to enter
tara bandu	to hang the prohibition
ulu (Waima'a)	area of rice field
uma andar	double or multistorey house
uma lulik	origin house
umane	fertility-givers
ume suba (Baikeno)	origin house
wani sedauk tama	the bees have not entered
ZEESM	special economic and social market zone (Oecusse and Atauro)

Audiovisual Resources

Film, video and photographs of many of the sites and ceremonies referred to in this book can be accessed through a digital archive of the cultural ecology of Timor-Leste. See:

Arkivu Dijitál Kultura no Ekolojia Timor-Leste (Cultural Ecology of Timor-Leste Digital Archive), accessed 25 June 2021, www.arkivukulturaekolojia.com.

The purpose of this collaborative archive is to document the knowledge and practices that connect ancestral house communities with their natural environment and cultural landscapes. It contains audiovisual material and documents about local histories, customs, languages and practices that bind people together in these house communities. See also:

Palmer, Lisa, *Wild Honey: Caring for Bees in a Divided Land*, Ronin Films, Arkivu Dijitál Kultura no Ekolojia Timor-Leste (Cultural Ecology of Timor-Leste Digital Archive), 2019, accessed 25 June 2021, arkivukulturaekolojia.com/waimata-films#/filmswild-honey/.

Palmer, Lisa and Susanna Barnes, *Holding Tightly: Custom and Healing in Timor-Leste*, Ronin Films, Arkivu Dijitál Kultura no Ekolojia Timor-Leste (Cultural Ecology of Timor-Leste Digital Archive), 2021, accessed 25 June 2021, arkivukulturaekolojia.com/waimata-films#/films-holding-tightly/.

Further Reading

The following works provide further elaborations on many of the themes introduced in this book:

Bovensiepen Judith, ed. *The Promise of Prosperity: Visions of the Future in Timor-Leste*. Canberra: ANU Press, 2018. doi.org/10.22459/PP.2018.

Carvalho, Demetrio do Amaral, ed. *Local Knowledge of Timor-Leste*. Jakarta: UNESCO, 2011. Accessed 10 November 2020, dev-chm.cbd.int/financial/micro/timor-local.pdf.

Commission for Reception, Truth and Reconciliation in East Timor. *Chega! Final Report of the Commission for Reception, Truth and Reconciliation in East Timor*. Dili: CAVR Timor-Leste, 2006. Accessed 9 November 2011, apo.org.au/node/676.

Damaledo, Andrey. *Divided Loyalties: Displacement, Belonging and Citizenship among East Timorese in West Timor*. Canberra: ANU Press, 2018. doi.org/10.22459/DL.09.2018.

Kehi, Balthasar. 'Nasib Seorang Asal Daerah Perbatasan Kolonial/The Fate of a Person from a Colonial Border'. In *Footsteps of Indonesians in Victoria* [Jejak Langkah Orang Indonesia di Victoria], edited by Tuti Gunawan and Iip Yahya, 447–61. Melbourne, IKAWIRIA (Indonesian Community Association of Victoria), 2016.

Kehi, Balthasar and Lisa Palmer. 'Hamatak Halirin: The Cosmological and Socio-Ecological Roles of Water in Koba Lima, Timor', *Bijdragen tot de Taal-, Land- en Volkenkunde* [Journal of the Humanities and Social Sciences of Southeast Asia] 168, no. 4 (2012): 445–71. doi.org/10.1163/22134379-90003552.

Langton, Marcia. 'Senses of Place'. Fourth Overland Lecture, 2001. *Overland* 166 (2002): 75–87.

McGrath, Kim. *Crossing the Line: Australia's Secret History in the Timor Sea*. Melbourne: Black Inc., 2017.

McWilliam, Andrew. *Post-Conflict Social and Economic Recovery in Timor-Leste: Redemptive Legacies*. New York: Routledge, 2020. doi.org/10.4324/9780429347948.

McWilliam, Andrew and Michael Leach, eds. *Routledge Handbook of Contemporary Timor-Leste*. New York: Routledge, 2019. doi.org/10.4324/9781315623177.

McWilliam, Andrew and Elizabeth Traube, eds. *Land and Life in Timor-Leste: Ethnographic Essays*, Canberra: ANU E Press, 2012. doi.org/10.22459/LLTL.12.2011.

Niner, Sara. *Xanana: Leader of the Struggle for Independent Timor-Leste*. Australian Scholarly Publishing, 2009.

Palmer, Lisa. 'The Cosmopolitics of Flow and Healing in North-Central Timor-Leste'. *The Australian Journal of Anthropology* 31, no. 2 (2020): 224–39. doi.org/10.1111/taja.12359.

Palmer, Lisa. 'Filmic Encounters: Multi-Species Care and Sacrifice on Island Timor'. *The Australian Journal of Anthropology* 32, no. 1 (2021): 80–95. doi.org/10.1111/taja.12381.

Palmer, Lisa. *Water Politics and Spiritual Ecology: Custom, Environmental Governance and Development*. New York: Routledge Explorations in Environmental Studies, 2015. doi.org/10.4324/9781315883250.

Palmer, Lisa and Andrew McWilliam. 'Ambivalent "Indigeneities" in an Independent Timor-Leste: Between the Customary and National Governance of Resources', *Asia Pacific Viewpoint* 59, no. 3 (2018): 265–75. doi.org/10.1111/apv.12197.

Peake, Gordon. *Beloved Land: Stories, Struggles, and Secrets from Timor-Leste*. Brunswick, Vic.: Scribe Publications, 2013.

Rose, Michael. *Indigenous Spirits and Global Aspirations in a Southeast Asian Borderland: Timor-Leste's Oecussi Enclave*. Amsterdam: Amsterdam University Press, 2020. doi.org/10.1515/9789048550340.

Trindade, Josh. *Josh Trindade: A Collection of Articles*. Beau Bassin, Mauritius: Lambert Academic Publishing, 2019.

Tsing, Anna. 'Cultivating the Wild: Honey-Hunting and Forest Management in Southeast Kalimantan'. In *Culture and the Question of Rights: Forests, Coasts, and Seas in Southeast Asia*, edited by C. Zerner, 24–55. London: Duke University Press, 2003. doi.org/10.1215/9780822383819-002.

www.ingramcontent.com/pod-product-compliance
Lightning Source LLC
Chambersburg PA
CBHW040154270326
41929CB00041B/3429